THE
LIGHT of SEX

THE
LIGHT OF SEX

INITIATION, MAGIC,
AND
SACRAMENT

MARIA DE NAGLOWSKA

Translated from the French with an
Introduction and Notes
by Donald Traxler

Inner Traditions
Rochester, Vermont • Toronto, Canada

Inner Traditions
One Park Street
Rochester, Vermont 05767
www.InnerTraditions.com

Originally published in French in 1932 under the title *La Lumière du Sexe* by Éditions de la Flèche

Illustrations by Lucien Helbé

Library of Congress Cataloging-in-Publication Data

Naglowska, Maria de, 1883-1936.
  [Lumière du sexe. English]
  The light of sex : initiation, magic, and sacrament / Maria de Naglowska ; translated from the French with an introduction and notes by Donald Traxler ; illustrations by Lucien Helbé.
      p. cm.
  "Originally published in French in 1932 under the title La lumière du sexe by Éditions de la Flèche"—T.p. verso.
  Includes bibliographical references and index.
  ISBN 978-1-59477-415-7 (pbk.)
  1. Sex—Miscellanea. 2. Magic. I. Traxler, Donald. II. Title.
  BF1623.S4N3413 2011
  155.3—dc22

                                                              2010048936

Printed and bound in the United States

10 9 8 7 6 5 4 3

Text design and layout by Priscilla Baker
This book was typeset in Garamond Premier Pro with Democratica used as a display typeface

You can't go back to your mother's womb to come out again with a new name, but you can again plunge into the woman who accepts you with love, to draw from her the Light that you are lacking.

MARIA DE NAGLOWSKA

CONTENTS

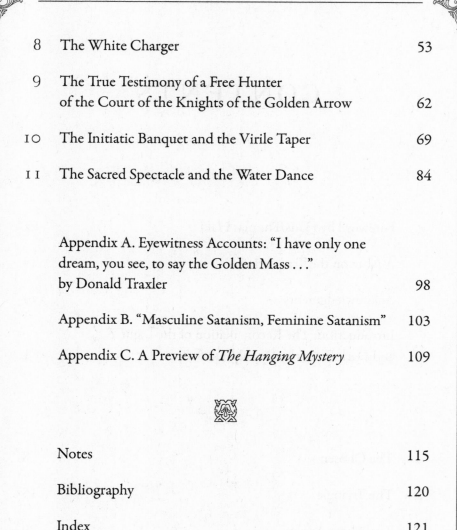

foreword

MARIA DE NAGLOWSKA

A PROTAGONIST OF SEXUAL MAGIC IN THE EARLY TWENTIETH CENTURY

Hans Thomas Hakl

Among the subjects guaranteed to evoke controversy and curiosity, it goes without saying that sexual magic will hold a prominent place. Due to the glaring absence of critical scholarly studies of this historical phenomenon much of the information available tends to be highly sensationalized and based on unreliable, secondhand sources.

One of the interesting aspects of conducting a critical study of sexual magic is how it brings us into contact with secret societies and initiatic orders, whose very nature makes them reluctant to provide their internal documents to outsiders. But the awakened interest in sex magic by practitioners of New Age pagan rituals has inspired a revival in this kind of research.[1]

In recent years the academic study of Western esotericism has generally been developing rapidly from a somewhat obscure specialty into a burgeoning professional field of scholarly activity and international organization. Once a domain restricted to the relatively secluded circles of specialists and hence hidden from the sight of most academic and non-academic readers, it is now becoming an increasingly popular topic of public and critical discussion in the context of journals, monographs, conferences, and scholarly organizations.[2]

In this context the translation and republication of the works of Maria de Naglowska is an enormous step in making the elusive information on sexual magic available to a new generation of readers.

The daughter of the province governor of Kazan, Maria de Naglowska (1883–1936) was born in St. Petersburg. There are several versions about her life, but the best-informed and most realistic source of information seems to be her pupil Marc Pluquet, who wrote her biography *La Sophiale*.[3] As a young man Pluquet lived in the anarchist and occultist milieus of Paris. When he met Maria de Naglowska he immediately fell under her spell, and later always referred to her as his spiritual mother.

Her early years were fraught with tragedy and loss. She was orphaned at the age of twelve when illness claimed her mother's life, her father having been murdered by a nihilist when she was still very young. She was then raised and educated in the prestigious Smolna Institute, a girl's school for the daughters of the impoverished nobility in Saint Petersburg. She also took classes in pedagogy at the Institute of the Order of Saint Catherine. According to René Thimmy (pseudonym of Maurice Magre) her mediumistic gifts were noted very early.[4] A persistent legend asserts she came into contact with Rasputin at this time. Others maintain that she was instead involved with the Khlisty sect, known for its sexual rites.

A rift occurred between her and her family when she fell in love with violinist Moise Hopenko and wanted to marry him. Her aristocratic relatives refused to bless a union with a Jewish commoner. This prompted the two lovers to leave Russia for Berlin, before settling in Geneva, where they married and had three children. Hopenko's passionate Zionism eventually prompted him to abandon Maria and their children around 1910. He left for Palestine where he became head of the Ron Shulamit Conservatory in Jaffa. According to Thimmy, Maria struggled to survive by teaching in private schools in Geneva and publishing several pedagogical works. She earned additional income as a translator while she also wrote poetry. Despite this she found time to pursue her studies at the University of Geneva and it is possible she earned a diploma—the nature of which is not known. She also worked as a journalist, but found herself imprisoned for her radical ideals. Following her release, she left Geneva for Berne and Basel but was eventually expelled from Switzerland and found refuge in Rome around 1920. Here, too, she found work as a journalist but, more importantly, Rome was where she cultivated her esoteric interests and met a Russian esoteric philosopher and Julius Evola, with whom she probably had a love affair. She and Evola are said to have co-authored the volume *La Parole Obscure du paysage intérieure: Poème a 4 voix.* Her next port of call was Alexandria where she lived with her son Alexandre. Still plying the trade of journalist, it was here she became a member of the Theosophical Society. After a brief return to Rome, she moved to Paris in 1929.

Denied a work permit, De Naglowska was forced to take up residence in a small Montparnasse hotel that was all that was affordable to one of her limited means. Montparnasse at this time was a hotbed for artists, political activists, and occultists of all stripes and she soon gained a reputation for her teachings on "Satanism" and sexual magic in these circles, whence her nickname "La Sophiale de Montparnasse." Her most ardent followers, whom she called the "Heirs of the Future"[5] included hermetic poet Claude d'Ygé (or Igée, pseudonym of Claude Lablatinière), the occult philosopher Jean Carteret, and the surrealist poet Camille Bryen.* She presided over daily meetings with a devoted circle of admirers in La Rotonde and La Coupole, the "cafés des occultistes," and Le Dôme, where she discussed her ideas and answered questions—speaking in all the languages in which she was fluent. She also met with disciples or important guests at the American Hotel on rue Bréa. Every Wednesday she gave public lectures in the Studio Raspail, 46 rue Vavin, where thirty or forty persons on average would gather to listen to her. Her disciple, "secretary," and friend Mister Dufour wrote down her conferences in stenography, but the whereabouts of these papers are unknown. Following these lectures, a much smaller group of select followers would retire to another room for sexual ritual work. What may come as a surprise to some is that she also visited the neighboring Roman Catholic Church of Notre-Dame des Champs every afternoon to spend time in contemplation. The two esoteric circles Maria de Naglowska was involved in at this time were the Confrérie de la Flèche d'Or (Fraternity of the Golden Arrow),

---

*The quite well-known French surrealist poet Ernest Gengenbach, who was in contact with André Breton, was also influenced by Maria de Naglowska, although she had left Paris before he could get to know her. Another person in favor with her teachings was the Swiss researcher and pioneer of homosexuality Camille Spiess.

which she had founded in 1932, and the Groupe des Polaires, which had an arithmetic oracle as its basis.

During this same period, De Naglowska published a journal, *La Flèche,* which would eventually number twenty issues in its three-year existence. The first issue contained an article written by Julius Evola. According to René Thimmy, whatever money she had—its origins were a mystery* as she granted her knowledge to her disciples for free—she invested it in her journal and the books she published. His description of her, whom he disguises under the name Vera de Petrouchka, is so different from popular concepts of a "Satanist":

> Somehow an atmosphere of purity, of chastity emanates from this small and quiet woman, who sat there modestly, speaking little and gesticulating even less and whose way of life seemed to be more or less ascetic. Her ordinary meals consisted of milk coffees and croissants or rolls. She practically never drank alcohol and her sole vice were some cigarettes.[6]

Although fairly modest or even nondescript in appearance, her blue eyes were often cited as an arresting feature, which Thimmy described as "blue and cold like a glacier or rather like the blades of daggers . . . lightened by a fire from within." This same author took pains to declare that although he did not fully trust her doctrines, he had full confidence in her sincerity and unselfishness. Several of her biographers emphasized her lack of venality and an aura of chastity that was seemingly at odds with the rituals she sponsored.

---

*It may have come from one of her sons.

Maria de Naglowska left Paris very suddenly in 1936 without naming any successor in her Confrérie. It has been speculated that this was possibly prompted by an accident to one of her followers during the rite of hanging, which she practiced in a higher degree. Marc Pluquet informs us that she went to Zurich to live with her daughter, Marie. It was there that she died in her bed on April 17, 1936, after allegedly having had a vision of her impending death in her magical mirror* in late 1935. But strangely enough someone (her daughter?) still remembered her there in 1974, when her book of poems *Malgré les Tempêtes . . . Chants d'Amour,* originally written 1921 in Rome, was reprinted privately in a very small number but in a luxurious design by the Grütli Druckerei in Zurich. And in 2009, seventeen of twenty issues of her extremely rare journal *La Flèche* were reprinted in Milan.

Hans Thomas Hakl received a Doctor of Law degree in 1970 and, together with partners, created a large international trading company as well as the publishing house Ansata in Switzerland, which specializes in the esoteric. After having sold his shares in both companies in 1996, he founded and is still co-editor of *Gnostika,* the most widely acknowledged German publication dealing with esotericism in an academic way. Hakl has collaborated in several international journals and dictionaries on the occult and religion and is the author of *Unknown Sources: National Socialism and the Occult* and *Eranos: An Alternative Intellectual History of the Twentieth Century.* His writings have been translated into English, French, Italian, Czech, and Russian.

---

*A photo of her magical mirror can be seen in the virtual Museum d'histoire surnaturelle (www.surnateum.org) founded by the French artist Fabrice Mignonneau in 1997. The keeper of the Department of Haunted Antiques, where the mirror is stored, is the famous Belgian art magician Christian Chelman.

A NOTE ON THE TRANSLATION

Maria de Naglowska often expressed herself in symbolic language. Some of this language was evidently intended to shock and to draw attention to herself and her teachings (two things not easily done in the vibrant and decadent Paris of the 1930s). My original plan was simply to translate this symbolic language into English and let it speak for itself. This is, indeed, what I have done in the translation. But I recently read a passage in Pluquet's biography in which Maria told her disciples that her teachings "would need to be translated into clear and accessible language for awakened women and men who would not necessarily be symbolists."[1] I knew then that Maria would want more. I have, therefore, included some explanatory expansions on the text in footnotes on the same page.

Maria de Naglowska had an aristocratic education, and her French was impeccable. She did not waste words or multiply them unnecessarily. Her writing style is chiseled and classical, worthy of a Voltaire or an Emerson. While I would not be capable of writing Naglowska's books, I have done my best to reproduce her style in these pages.

I have also tried in this translation to transmit Maria de Naglowska's vision, unencumbered by the nonsense that has been written about her by some. It is a magnificent vision, with the potential to uplift those who share it.

ACKNOWLEDGMENTS

My gratitude is due to many people, whose contributions have been as diverse as they themselves. Among those who have passed away, it is first due to Mariya Naglovskaya, Maria de Naglowska herself, whose guiding presence I often seemed to feel as I was doing the work. I am grateful also to her favorite student, Marc Pluquet, whom I regard as a spiritual brother. Among the living, I am grateful for the friendship of Philippe Pissier, Matthieu Leon, Jean-Pierre Passalacqua, and many others who offered assistance, advice, criticism, or moral support. I must thank Hans Thomas Hakl for being so kind as to write the foreword to this book. Endless thanks are due to many wonderful people at Inner Traditions, including Jon Graham, Kelly Bowen, Maria Murray-Urdaneta, Kristi Tate, Jeanie Levitan, Erica Robinson, Peri Ann Swan, and my project editor, Mindy Branstetter. These and many others worked smoothly and professionally as a team to produce this book. Last but not least, I would like to thank Sandy Shaw, my wife, for patiently waiting for me to come up for air from my studying, translating, and writing. I thank everyone for their contributions. If there are shortcomings or errors, they are my own and I take full responsibility for them. Mariya, this book is for you.

INTRODUCTION

THE RECONCILIATION OF THE
LIGHT AND DARK FORCES

Donald Traxler

I n 1931 there was an article in the Paris edition of the *Chicago Tribune** that spoke of an attractive Russian woman, Maria de Naglowska, who was selling her own little newspaper, *La Flèche,* on the streets of Montparnasse. Dark magic was imputed to her, and it was said that her followers met weekly in a large room that lacked decoration, to practice some gentle experiments. All of this was chalked up to a survival of nineteenth-century romanticism.

Apparently the experiments were not always so mild, because they may have included erotic, ritual hanging. Far from being representative of nineteenth-century romanticism, these sessions are said to have been attended by the avant-garde and the notorious of the time, including Man Ray, William Seabrook, Michel

---

*Tuesday, November 3, 1931, page 4.

Leiris, Georges Bataille, and André Breton. Jean Paulhan, for whom *L'Histoire d'O* was written, is also said to have attended.* We know that surrealist poet and painter Camille Bryen was a member of Naglowska's group, as the writer Ernest Gengenbach appears to have been, and it seems significant that one of the best studies of Naglowska was done by another surrealist, Sarane Alexandrian.[1]

Who was this strange woman who peddled her newspaper on the streets of Montparnasse?

Maria de Naglowska was born in St. Petersburg in 1883, the daughter of a prominent Czarist family.†[2] She went to the best schools and received the best education that a young woman of the time could get. She fell in love with a young Jewish musician, Moise Hopenko, and married him against the wishes of her family. The rift with Maria's family caused the young couple to leave Russia, going to Germany and then to Switzerland. After Maria had given birth to three children, her young husband, a Zionist, decided to leave his family and go to Palestine. This made things very difficult for Naglowska, who was forced to take various jobs as a journalist to make ends meet. While she was living in Geneva she also wrote a French grammar for Russian immigrants to Switzerland. Unfortunately, Naglowska's libertarian ideas tended to get her into trouble with governments wherever she went. She spent most of

---

*I have not yet been able to trace these often-made claims to reliable, original sources. In the meantime, they should be regarded as hearsay.

†I have drawn most of the details about Naglowska's life from the short biography titled *La Sophiale,* written by her favorite student, Marc Pluquet. It is, by far, the most reliable source.

the 1920s in Rome, and at the end of that decade, she moved on to Paris.

While in Rome, Maria de Naglowska met Julius Evola, a pagan traditionalist who wanted to reinstate the pantheon of ancient Rome. Evola was also an occultist, being a member of the Group of Ur and counting among his associates some of the followers of Giuliano Kremmerz. It is said that Naglowska and Evola were lovers. It is known, at least, that they were associates for a long time. She translated one of his poems into French (the only form in which it has survived), and he translated some of her work into Italian.

While occultists give a great deal of weight to Naglowska's relationship with Evola, it is clear that there must have been other influences. Some believe that she was influenced by the Russian sect of the Khlysti, and some believe that she knew Rasputin (whose biography she translated). Maria, though, gave the credit for some of her unusual ideas to an old Catholic monk whom she met in Rome. Although Maria said that he was quite well known there, he has never been identified.[3]

Maria said that the old monk gave her a piece of cardboard, on which was drawn a triangle to represent the Trinity. The first two apices of the triangle were clearly labeled to indicate the Father and the Son. The third, left more indistinct, was intended to represent the Holy Spirit. To Maria, the Holy Spirit was feminine. We don't know how much was the monk's teaching and how much was hers, but Maria taught that the Father represented Judaism and Reason, while the Son represented Christianity, the Heart, and an era whose end was approaching. To Maria, the feminine Spirit represented a

New Era, sex, and the reconciliation of the light and dark forces in nature.

It is mostly this idea of the reconciliation of the light and dark forces that has gotten Maria into trouble and caused her to be thought of as a Satanist. Maria herself is partly responsible for this, having referred to herself as a "Satanic Woman" and used the name also in other ways in her writings. Evola, in his book *The Metaphysics of Sex,* mentioned her "deliberate intention to scandalize the reader."[4] Here is what Naglowska herself had to say about it:

> *Nous défendons à nos disciples de s'imaginer Satan (= l'esprit du mal ou l'esprit de la destruction) comme vivant en dehors de nous, car une telle imagination est le propre des idolâtres; mais nous reconnaissons que ce nom est vrai.*

> We forbid our disciples to imagine Satan (= the Spirit of Evil or the Spirit of Destruction) as living outside of us, for such imagining is proper to idolaters; but we recognize that this name is true.

In 1929 Naglowska moved to Paris, where she got the unwelcome news that she would not be given a work permit. Deprived of the ability to be employed in a regular job, she would have to depend on her own very considerable survival skills. She began work on the book for which she is best known today, her "translation" of *Magia Sexualis* by Paschal Beverly Randolph.[5] This work by the American hermetist and sex theorist is known only in Naglowska's "translation." I have put the word "translation" in quotation marks because it is really a compilation. Only about two-thirds of the work can be identified as being from Randolph. The rest is from sources only beginning to be identified, or from Naglowska herself, and the organization of the material is clearly her contribution as well.

While Naglowska was working on *Magia Sexualis,* she began giving lectures or "conferences" on an original teaching of her own. She called it the Doctrine of the Third Term of the Trinity. Her "conferences" were at first often held in cafés. The proprietors of these venues were pleased with the influx of patrons and often gave Maria free food and coffee. In a short time her following grew to the point where she could afford to rent the large, undecorated room (mentioned in the *Chicago Tribune* article above and in Pluquet's *La Sophiale*) for private meetings, which held thirty to forty people.*[6] It was thus that Maria survived.

Maria's income was supplemented by her publishing endeavors. After the 1931 publication of *Magia Sexualis,* Naglowska turned

---

*According to Pluquet, there were only thirty to forty people in the hall when it was full, and the overflow stood in a *baie vitrée,* or glassed-in bay, that separated the hall from the entrance. The hall in question was the old Studio Raspail at 46 Rue Vavin (not to be confused with the present cinema on Bd. Raspail). The building now houses an Italian restaurant that has a capacity of 120 seats. The space may have been enlarged, or it may not. The low divider that formed the baie vitrée is still there, but it no longer seems to have glass over it. It would take a sizable crowd to fill the space and still have overflow standing in the entryway. On page 14 Pluquet states that all these "conferences" were taken down in shorthand by a certain Mr. Dufour. Unfortunately, these shorthand notes have not yet surfaced.

to writing original works. One of these, *Le Rite sacré de l'amour magique,* a metaphysical novelette apparently containing elements of her own life, was published as a supplement to her street newspaper in early 1932, having earlier been serialized in her newspaper.[7] The little newspaper, to which she and other occultists contributed, was called *La Flèche, Organe d'Action Magique.* It was the public voice of her magical group, *La Confrérie de la Flèche d'Or.*

The book on which the present work is based, *La Lumière du sexe,* was published in late 1932.[8] It was the first of two works (the other was *Le Mystère de la pendaison,*[9] or The Hanging Mystery) that were required reading for initiation into *La Flèche d'Or.*[10] These books are now quite rare. To my knowledge, neither they nor any of Naglowska's other original works have ever before been translated into English.

Maria de Naglowska is said to have been very psychic. She predicted the calamity of the Second World War,[11] and in 1935 she had a dream presaging her own death.[12] Knowing that she was going to die, she refused to reprint *The Light of Sex* and *The Hanging Mystery,* which had both sold out. She told her followers that nothing would be able to be done to spread her teachings for two or three generations.[13] She went to live with her daughter in Zurich, and it was there that she died, at the age of fifty-two, on April 17, 1936.

It is clear to me, having now read four of Naglowska's books and most of what she wrote in her little newspaper, that she was not a Satanist. She was, on the other hand, a mystic, a philosopher, and a superb writer. I shall be happy if the present trans-lation, part of a projected series of such translations, makes her known and accessible to a wider audience than she has heretofore had. Maria de Naglowska's writings have spoken strongly and with great vitality to me, and it is my belief that they will speak so to many others.

DONALD TRAXLER began working as a professional translator (Benemann Translation Service, Berlitz Translation Service) in 1963. Later, he did translations for several institutions in the financial sector. On his own time he translated poetry and did his first metaphysical translations in the early 1980s. He later combined these interests, embarking on an ambi-tious, multi-year project to translate the works of Lalla (also known as Lalleshvari, or Lal Ded), a beloved fourteenth-century poet of Kashmir Shaivism. That project is still not complete, but many of the translations have become favorites of contemporary leaders of the sect. He is currently focusing on Western mysticism, and is halfway through a four-book series on Maria de Naglowska for Inner Traditions. He is contemplating a major project on another European mystic and an eventual return to and com-pletion of the Lalla project. Except for Lalla, he translates from Spanish, French, and Italian. All of his projects are labors of love.

THE CHOSEN

*It is necessary to do the difficult
and to try the impossible*

To understand the doctrine of the Third Term of the Trinity, it is necessary right in the beginning to get rid of the idea that there is anything in the Universe, visible or invisible, that is absolute, perfect, immobile.

This idea, which has held sway in our minds for too long, has falsified human reasoning, and it keeps us from recognizing Truth.

Imbued, consciously or unconsciously, with Catholic dogmas, our spiritual thinkers imagine that the Divine, unlike the human, is unchangeable and perfect.

Thus they oppose earthly nature to heavenly nature, digging an abyss between Man and God, between matter and spirit, and obliging individuals desirous of attaining the "higher regions" to nourish in their hearts absurd aspirations, of which the immediate consequence is the veil of hypocrisy extending over the reality of our lives.

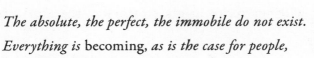

The absolute, the perfect, the immobile do not exist.
Everything is becoming, *as is the case for people,*
animals, plants.
God is not "He who is," but "He who was, who is, and
who eternally will be."
God is Life. God is living, mobile.

To familiarize oneself with our doctrine, it is this dogma that it is necessary first of all to understand.

But what is a dogma?

These days the word gives rise to a disagreeable feeling in plenty of otherwise strong minds.

One attaches to the word an imperative meaning that obscures its real sense, which is, however, still clear, and one wants nothing at all to do with it, because one wants to be free!

Still, in its primitive purity the word *dogma* didn't mean anything other than teaching, always with this difference, that it implied the idea of a greater precision than the profane term that one uses today without distaste.

Now, what is teaching, if not formulating an idea in a precise and clear way?

Teaching does not mean convincing, and still less, giving orders.

To teach is to propose exact formulas, which each person is free to accept or reject; but when the teaching is proposed in dogmas, one will not separate its content from the words.

One will not recite in one's own way the idea accepted or rejected.

That is the virtue of the dogma: it is the best formula for the expression of the idea conceived.

Therefore you will not translate our thought otherwise than thus:

The doctrine of the Third Term of the Trinity recognizes and honors the only living God: Life.

No one is obligated to bow down before our words without examination, but no one will be our disciple unless they formulate our theses as we do ourselves; for at the time of writing it is not a matter of uniting a large number under the flag of "La Flèche," but of communicating to a small nucleus the exact sense of the new teaching.

Today humanity can be compared to a long line of railroad cars that a Divine Locomotive is pulling on the rails of a narrow, dark tunnel.

The locomotive and the first cars are already leaving the tunnel, while the rest of the train is still in the shadows.

It is necessary for the accelerators of the train, the elite of humanity, to be initiated into the new doctrine if one wants all of humanity, or at least the majority, to arrive at the Light before the catastrophe of the end of the Second Era.

This end is approaching, for the Dark Era can only last for a limited time.

A great mercy has permitted the shadowy passage, but those who arrive too late will perish under the Mountain when it collapses.

Let us make haste, it is time!

But to whom are we directing our words?

Where shall we find persons capable of accelerating the movement of things?

It is certain that the individuals who are currently governing on Earth cannot do anything. They are the slaves and not the leaders of the masses.

None, among those who currently find themselves at the head of a human organization, whatever it may be, can lead the masses where they wish to, but rather they must direct themselves where the masses are pushing them.

For there exists, in our "modern" time, an opinion that is called public and which is the principal determining factor of collective actions.

It is true that by clever detours, through the press and by other channels, one manages to move the masses in order to get from them the desired agreement, but one does not achieve this except with the strictly necessary condition of allowing the people to believe that none of the principles that are dear to them have been disturbed, even when appearances testify otherwise.

In other words—cruder and more brutal—one might well say that the current leaders of all nations cannot impose their will upon the masses except on condition of fooling them.

We do not wish, here, to critique this state of affairs, but we believe that strict logic permits us to conclude that the people who are currently armed with what is called "power" are not those who can do anything in the area of modifying the very principles that hold sway in the minds of the masses.

> *They are not, consequently, the elite to which we are*
> *   directing ourselves . . .*
> *Neither is the crowd the elite, that goes without*
> *   saying.*
> *The crowd is a blind mass that likes or detests, but*
> *   never thinks.*

Its current "opinion" is made up of the remains of old dogmas, the light of which has been lost since the human train entered under the arch of the tunnel—symbol of the Dark Era—after which the new countryside begins.

The crowd no longer believes in the God of the Second Era, the Christ-Savior, but it holds on to the ethics, because it needs to know which human act belongs to "good" and which to "bad," and no one has yet come to tell it anything new on this subject.

It is not that the crowd takes any great care to act according to the "good," but it experiences an imperative need to safeguard its homogeneity because a Law, of which it is unaware but which acts in it constantly, desires that every human river should stay in its bed and that the drops that compose it—the individuals—should all flow together toward the same unknown end.

The masses do not accept that one of their own should appear to be different from them. They need for all to act in the same manner, and it is because of this that the line between "good" and "bad" is indispensable to them.

A Divine Law, stronger than all human reasoning, wishes it to be so.

It is, therefore, not to the crowds that we shall direct ourselves.

We shall speak to those—very rare ones—who do not govern and who themselves are not governed at all.

To those who live on the margin of modern society, not having found any place for themselves in the old home.

Those are the ones who belong to the future, because their spirit is virgin: they have not contracted any earthly marriage and have not sworn fidelity to any thing of the past.

Those are the ones who wait—to grow—that a new flame may be ignited in their heart.

The profane say of those persons that they have been disinherited. But we say that they are the heirs to the future.

It is in them that the active force will be formed that will draw the human river into a new bed—in the triumphant era of the Third Term of the Trinity.

They will understand this book and will retain its theses by heart.

Deep in their beings, these theses will put forth new branches, and a harmonious foliage will crown the Plant.*

The new Tree will appear then on the Earth in all its splendor, humanity will eat of its fruits, and Day and Night will be changed:

---

*Naglowska described this "Plant" elsewhere as "the Human Tree."

for the crowd, other acts will carry the names "good" and "bad." Other principles will inspire the actions of people, and another Light will be recognized.

This will be the work of the elite to which we dedicate these pages.

THE TRIANGLE

We have proclaimed since the first page of this book that God is Life.

We could also say that Life is God, for these two propositions are equivalent.

But, whether one adopts one or the other of these formulas, it is a serious matter, and misunderstandings are possible.

Be prudent, then, and do not accept this dogma without a long preliminary meditation.

Do not declare yourselves convinced until, starting from these three words, "Life is God," you feel yourself drawn into a depth where words cease to apply.

If your meditation leads you on the right Path, you will get a shudder of horror from it, for it is with this terrible sensation that the Initiate recognizes having touched the Divine.

He who has done this, he who has put his finger into the Heart, into the Center of Universal Life (= God), no longer speaks as others, and if he told what he knows, no one would believe him.

For nothing is the same from above as it appears from below.

The hermetic saying, which seems to proclaim the contrary, actually means this: "You will not know a thing from below unless you first see the thing from above, for, in spite of your erroneous understanding, what you see as a negative on Earth is an analog of its positive correspondence in the Origin."

It is therefore impossible to know Truth by means of patient analysis of phenomena from down here, but one could know the Reason and the Truth of each detail of the visible world by first projecting oneself into the very soul of the Universe (= God).

Never will humanity be able to do this, for if they could, as the two opposites touched, there would result the neutrality of Life itself, that is to say, the annihilation of God.

But he who was, who is, and who will be, abides eternally!

He has created since the beginning—which never was—Heaven and Earth, that is to say, Truth and the Lie, the reality of the Origin, and the fallacy of Appearance, and when he breathed into mankind, "created in his image," the capacity to know the mystery of Creation, He immediately forbade them to enjoy the fruit of the Tree of the Knowledge of Good and Evil, which vivifies this capacity.

For if mankind had eaten this fruit, God (= Life) would no longer exist.

This would have been the triumph of the absurd.

But the absurd does not exist within Truth.

But neither is it necessary that men, lost in their false light, should turn aside too much from Truth. This is why, from time to time, in predetermined periods called "Dark Ages," an Emissary of Heaven speaks to mankind. Humans never understand what the Emissary says to them, but they approach the Emissary's Light, captivated by the magical charm that emanates from it.

Then, a new religion is given to Earth, and humans reorganize themselves in conformity with the Law.

A link is then formed between Truth and human Reason: a sacred art symbolizing what the masses are not able to understand.

One inaugurates rites and Masses that dramatize for the profane the great principles according to which Life (= God) is explained and ordered.

From this art and from the Initiates who realize it, a force passes through the masses. Each individual receives from it what he can.

The totality of society gains thereby in harmony and in Light, and all of humanity distances itself from the bestial (unaware) state and approaches the angelic (aware) state.

But people will not be angels. There is a formal Law there.

The Fall of him who raises himself is obligatory at the very instant when he reaches the Summit.

For God wants to live, and not to die. Life (= God) is living.

There you see the terrifying thing that he recognizes who arrives at God.

There you see the inevitable Law of Death, there you see the symbol of the Hanged Man (twelfth arcanum of the Tarot).

Now you will understand the necessity of the Passion of the

Christ, the renouncement of the great Moses before the gates of the promised land, and you will know why, when a church arrives at its apogee, reanimating the magical faith in all, it determines by itself, and by the conscious will of its chiefs, its own decadence. It lessens, little by little, the grace that it dispenses, until it is reduced to nothing.

At Noon, the Sun must again take up its course toward Midnight.

Therefore, blessed are those who watch in the dark hours of the Night of the Ages.

Blessed are those who, under the black roof,* are the first to hear the Awakening call, announcing the true renaissance of the spirit.

Those are the chosen ones who force the human river to bend back upon itself and to correct the Angle,† thanks to which the Lie draws near to the Truth, leaving along the Way the debris of the used crust.‡

The chosen ones cannot be numerous, for the magical charge projected upon the Earth at the decisive moment is counted parsimoniously.

There are few places at the triumphal banquet. Watch, open your eyes, if you wish to take part in the feast.

Behold: *the Bridegroom will come soon, because the Bride is ready.*

---

*The roof of the tunnel through which humanity's train is passing (see previous chapter).
†Of the cyclical Triangle.
‡Of the riverbank.

She will be the first to enter the Temple of Awakening, and her friends will enter with her.

Group yourselves around the Bride, if you wish to have your share of the Illumination that is announced.

The instant having passed, equilibrium will be reestablished, and the Lie, weakened, will take up its course toward the new Noon, and from there to the next Night.

There are thus three of these times . . . eternally!

Is it Night? It is the formation of an Angle.

Is it Noon? It is the point where the straight line comes closest to the Center (= the Divine Eye).*

Is it Evening? Humanity distances itself again from the Truth . . . until the new Midnight, until the new Awakening . . .

And the Angles of this eternal course are three—the supreme symbol of the Truth has the form of a Triangle.

Understanding this is of capital importance.

---

*The Eye in the Triangle.

THE THREE
ANGLES

We wrote at the beginning of this book that heavenly nature (Divine Nature) is similar to terrestrial nature (to the nature of mankind, animals, plants), but in the chapter titled "The Triangle," we have drawn the reader into the contrary idea, declaring that the Lie will never be able to rejoin the Truth: they will approach each other and distance themselves from each other incessantly.

This apparent paradox is explained in the following way:

The Lie, the error, the contradiction, lives in human Reason because it is human Reason that protests Day and Night against God (= Life). Having bitten into the apple that gives the Knowledge of Good and Evil, a great shame came over the first Man, and he hastened to cover the sex of his Woman as well as his own, preferring Shadow to the Light.

The triangular course began again at that moment . . .

Were Adam and Eve the first people? Was there a world before them?

The Creation in six days, as Genesis tells it to us, is it true, or is it a poem?

The doctrine of the Third Term of the Trinity answers these questions thus:

Nothing else is true except that which is presented in the form of a poem, for what is absolutely true for human Reason is false by definition, since we have said that the characteristic of Reason is to spread the Lie.

The history told in Genesis is true just because Reason will never be able to content itself with it at all.

It is said there that on the first day—which never was—God created the Light.

On the second day, after the first night, he separated the Heavens from the Earth.

On the third day, he ordered the waters to detach themselves from the continents and to clasp them as a mother would her children. Plants came out of the belly of the Earth and extended their branches toward Heaven.

The fourth day saw the appearance of the Sun, the Moon, and all the stars.

Still another night followed, a night which had its light, and on the fifth day birds sang in the air, while mute fish populated the waters.

After the fifth day, came the sixth day: the creation of animals that walk on paws and the creation of the Man, who gave to each thing its name.

All that is perfectly true, because all that confirms the eternal Law of the Triangle, stating precisely its three successive Angles:

The departure point—nonexistent—where perfect Light reigns; Heaven and Earth, forming the first Angle of the Base after the first shadows; the second Angle of the Base formed by the separation of the waters and determining the line of the elevation to the meeting of the Light, symbolized by the plants.

The first Triangle is thus completed.

The first?

There never was a first, but it is necessary to speak of it to men, because of the Lie of their Reason.

You will learn the falsified language when you come down from the Mountain to speak to the sons of the Earth.

After the formation of the first Triangle, the Fall recommences, the Fall of the Light, symbolized henceforth by multiple planets which rise and fall in the sky, each at its Noon.

The Fall lasts until the first song of the birds, separated by the Earth from the silence of the fish. Then the first Angle of the Base is formed again, and in the night, which has its Light (the baseline of the Triangle), the course continues.

At the sixth day of Creation, the animals that walk on their paws and the Man, who recognizes his Woman, symbolize the Angle of the renewal and redetermine the line of the elevation now symbolized by the Child.

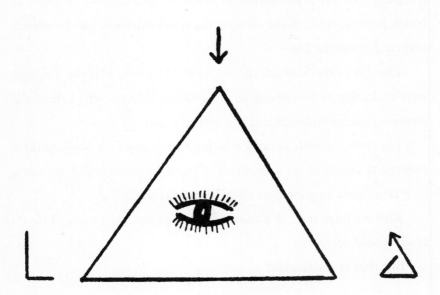

The Three Hypostases: the Father, the Son, the Mother.
The Three Signs: the Rod, the Cross, the Arrow.
The Three Acts: Birth, Struggle, Triumph.

The seventh day—which does not exist for Life (= God), which never rests—is a concession granted to mankind.

This is why Moses ordained that the Sabbath be celebrated, proclaiming that no work should be done on that day by the sons of Israel, because work is the slavery, the condemnation, the penitence inflicted upon the Lie.

The day of the Sabbath should be lived by men as if the Triangle were no longer in movement, as if the Great Voyage—the Life of the Universe—were finished and the end attained.

This concession is necessary to human Reason, for how would it consent to continue its vain effort of protestation if it did not seem to it from time to time that its will could triumph?

And we have said: if Reason did not protest any more, Life (= God) would cease.

But that is impossible!

Now reread this chapter, "The Three Angles," and learn by heart the following dogma:

You will not be an idolater!

You will know that nothing can represent God (= Life) in an adequate fashion: neither your thought that draws you on high, nor your Heart that guards you on Earth, nor your vital instinct that pushes you into the depth of the womb of the Earth.

You will abstain, consequently, from all profane art, but you will fix your attention on the sacred symbols whose virtue is to endlessly point out to you your ignorance.

REASON

H aving meditated on the things written in the preceding pages, the anxious disciple asks himself this question:

"Is human Reason so powerful that God himself should have any cause to fear it?" "Can Man—so small a creature—be a menace to the whole Universe?" "What is this strange enigma?"

Here is the teaching of the doctrine of the Third Term of the Trinity on this subject:

To penetrate into the heart of the mysteries, everything must be considered in its symbolic sense, and Man, whose three sacred points (the Three Angles) are found respectively in the head, in the Heart, and in the organ that one does not name because one is ignorant of its Light,*[1] symbolizes, in himself, the totality of Life (= God).

---

*Strangely, there is light associated with the vulvar area in females. This was pointed out by MacDonald and Margolese in *Fertility and Sterility* 1:26 (1950). They reported that irradiation of the vulva with near-ultraviolet light results in luminescence unique to this area. Since all living tissues fluoresce, I'm not sure what they meant by "unique." This particular fluorescence is of different colors and intensities depending on such factors as menarche, menstruation, pregnancy, and menopause. Whatever it may mean, it's interesting.

Each bit of the visible world is not a part of God (= Life), but a complete symbol of the latter.

The totality is in each particle, and each particle reflects all, for Life (= God) sports there in fullness.

Modern people conceive of that with difficulty, because they have acquired the habit of ignoring Life (= God) and studying only Death (= its/his Shadow).

But we are not addressing ourselves to the "modern" human.

The anxious disciple—he who interests us—will understand, instead, that human Reason, in spite of the infinitely small place that it occupies in the immensity of the Universe, is at the same time, by itself, the whole danger, for total destructive power resides in its fullness in each brain.

We forbid our disciples to imagine Satan (= the Spirit of Evil or the Spirit of Destruction) as living outside ourselves, for such imagining is proper to idolaters,* but we recognize that the name is true.

We shall say therefore that Reason is in the service of Satan. We shall also say that it is Satan, because Day and Night it protests, like him, against Life (= God).

Reason must protest—we have already said it—because, if it did not continue to protest, Life (= God) would not continue to be. But this obligation is at the same time a Calvary for it.

---

*This is an extremely important passage, and we will have several occasions to refer back to it. Naglowska often does so herself, with the shorthand form, "Do not be an idolater."

Here we touch on one of the greatest mysteries, carefully hidden by the Initiates in the secret doctrines of the Royal Art: the Calvary of Satan!* . . . Follow us well, while chasing any idolatrous imagination† out of your mind.

Satan (= Reason) can do everything, but it will never do anything completely.

It is what God is: Life, but in the inverse sense. That is why its action tends toward destruction.

The destruction of the visible world, that is to say of the Manifestation of Life (= God), appears to its desire as the very condition of its liberation.

It is because of this that it struggles Day and Night against God (= Life).

Its total liberation will never be attained, but if it ceased to destroy what it does destroy, all the dynamism spread throughout the world would stop, and Nothingness would reign.

The negative action of Satan is therefore absolutely necessary to God (= Life), just as his continual deception. There you have the tragedy of the Royal Art!

Meanwhile, those who devote themselves to it do eminently priestly work, and those who persevere, climbing toward the Summit, are the Sacrificers of themselves. For well before attaining the Summit, the Initiate knows that up there he will be hanged (twelfth arcanum of the Tarot).

---

*Which is also the Calvary of Reason, a very important point.
†This is one of Naglowska's shorthand admonitions to us not to imagine Satan as living outside ourselves.

There is no Initiate who does not serve Satan*[2] before serving God, for it is only at the supreme moment of the Fall from the Summit that the Royal Art, exercised by the disciple, ceases to be Satanic and becomes Divine.[†]

And one will not fall from the Peak before having arrived there!

O disciple! You who are disturbed by things, will you ask us whether Christ himself served Satan before serving God, his Father?

And would you like to know whether the great Moses followed the same Calvary?

Yes . . . we say Yes, because it is the Truth.

The Son of God (= the Son of Man) had to suffer and be hanged, in order to cast back upon all men the power which, kept in his illumined brain, would have infallibly meant the annihilation of the world, of Life, of God.

---

*I interpret this to mean Satan as the Will to Die or the Opposer of Life (which represents control and proper, intentional—sacred—use of sex). In the ascensional part of the Triangle, before the Summit is reached, this Negator or denier of Life (within us) is to be regenerated or reformed to become part of humanity's ascent. But serving Satan also means serving Reason (as Naglowska has previously explained). The ascensional part of the Triangle, like climbing the slope of the initiatic Mountain, is the Calvary of Reason. This is the Path of Knowledge (*Jñanamarga* in Hinduism), which leads to Illumination if one perseveres in it, but is not itself Illumination.

†That Maria de Naglowska had herself achieved Illumination is suggested by the following quotation from *La Flèche:* "Nous n'allons pas vers l'Unité, nous sommes l'Unité dès l'origine qui ne fut jamais" (We are not going toward Unity, we are Unity since the beginning that never happened). This statement shows Maria to have been a nondualist. This is the full Upanishadic realization, achieved within a Western setting. For this, if nothing else, Naglowska deserves an important place in the history of religion. For a nondualist, belief in or worship of Satan as something outside of the Self would be idolatry. So it would have been for Maria.

Meditate on that, O anxious disciple, if you want us to tell you more, but reflect now on the great wisdom of the incomparable Moses, who commanded the children of Israel to ignore the true name of God.

You, who guess it now, do not abuse it!

THE HEART

The Heart receives and sends out blood.

The Heart receives every drop of blood contained in your body. It expels them all, without distinction.

The great virtue of the Heart is Balance.

Do you know, O disciple, what Balance is?

You have seen a set of scales at rest. Have you reflected upon this symbol full of serious instruction?

Do you believe that it is necessary to love? No, because love generates hate.

Do you believe that it is necessary to have pity? No, because from pity is born cruelty.

Do you believe that it is necessary to be enthusiastic? No, because from enthusiasm comes desolation.

As you climb the steep slope of the Mountain, you will learn that Justice is greater than love, because Justice is Balance.

Justice inspires one to acts of love where hate is too strong, but it unleashes hatred where love abuses.

Justice is merciful when cruelty rages, but it is cruel when pity is loose.

Justice fills human hearts with joy when desolation is too great, but it tortures people and causes tears when joy overflows.

Justice is calm, implacable, lucid. It is proper to those who are purified, those who, armed with an iron will, have learned to conquer all their own impatiences: the impatience of anger, the impatience of amorous passion, the impatience of various appetites, the impatience of all forms of pride.

Those are the main realities. They dominate the crowds, and the crowds obey them. They straighten the Path of God (= Life) when Night becomes too dark. At Midnight they launch the call to the Return, and everything that is not definitively dead follows them without revolt.

O disciples: Be strong and numerous at this Third Turning of the Road,* at which we have arrived!

What is the relationship between Justice, on the one hand, and God (= Life) and Satan (= Reason) on the other?

Which of the two is just, which of the two is the Just? One tends toward Life, the other tends toward Death. Is it better that the Universe should live, or is it preferable that it should disappear?

It is not given to us to choose between these two alternatives: Justice belongs to the stronger one, because that is the one that imposes its Law.

---

*At this Third Angle of the cyclical Triangle.

The Law is the triumphant Will of the Stronger One.

Meditate on that, O disciple, before listening to the cries of your sentiments.

Forget everything, imagine the abstract presence of Yes and No, as if the visible world did not exist.

In the frozen waste of Nothingness and in the indifference of a sky with neither Moon nor Sun, nor the many stars, imagine the solitary duel between Yes and No.

If No triumphed, if it was the stronger, would it do you any good to say that it was unjust?

And if Yes is the winner, what can you do except obey?

Now, Yes (Life = God) is the winner, since we are here to discuss it.

Death cedes to Life, since the world continues to exist.

And even if you wanted to make it disappear, you could not.

The will to live (Life = God) triumphs eternally over the will to die. This is why it dictates its Law, and it is why its Law is just.

Relearn this:

You will honor your father and your mother who have given you
    life, and you will have your recompense on Earth. This rec-
    ompense will be eternal if you have any children;
you will not kill, because everything must live, and you will not
    prevent any animal from serving Justice;
you will not commit adultery, because it is necessary that every
    son should know his father;
and since it is necessary that your son should be able to honor

you, conform yourself to the rules of decency established in the human city to which you belong:

do not steal, for it is necessary that each man should nourish himself and nourish his children;

do not bear false witness, for it is necessary that the judges should know to what to adhere in human quarrels;

do not cause trouble in human affairs by jealousies and unworthy envies. Your neighbor's wife is his, therefore do not covet her. The animals are his, therefore do not touch them. His house, his land, and all his other goods, moral or concrete, are his, therefore do not concern yourself with them.

Be kind to your neighbor, but do not accept harm.

O disciple! We confirm, as you see, the strict Law of Moses, because we recognize that he was the Man of God (= of Life), and that in him reigned Balance.

Do not pardon, but do not exact vengeance yourselves!

In a well-ordered society there are courts, and one does not confer the title of judge on a man whose passions are excessive.

This is the Law of God (= Life).

The man who climbs the initiatic Mountain always turns away from God, away from Life, away from Balance, and consequently away from Justice.

Moses himself struggled against God!

That is why we said in the chapter titled "Reason" that the

Initiate who climbs the dangerous slope of the Mountain obeys Satan up to the Summit.

Satan promises his disciple to keep him from falling from the Peak, or at least he says to him, "You will fall, but you will stay alive!"—but the duly initiated disciple knows that Hanging is indispensable up there, for only thus does the Light fall upon all, to the glory of God (= Life).

This is why, O disciple, before undertaking the formidable ascent of Reason (= Satan), you should place the true spirit of the Law of Moses in your Heart.

Do not exaggerate anything. Be calm and well disposed. Develop within yourself the great virtue of the Heart: Balance.

SEX

When Balance reigns within you, and "your left is as your right," climb the initiatic Mountain, and search out the mystery of Life.

Seek out the Woman—Eve—and ask her for the apple that grants the Knowledge of Good and Evil.

Definitely do not address yourself to the blind woman who, silently, accomplishes her task as mother.

That one obeys God (= Life) and cares little about the Human Revolution. Don't bother her! Let her tend to her children.

Address yourself to the other—she exists!—to whom Satan has confided his secret.

Since the beginning of the world, she has been waiting at the very Heart of God (= Life) for the morning hour when she will be permitted to speak.

But here a teaching is called for, a dogma that we state as follows:

From the struggle between God (= Will to Live) and Satan (= Will to Die), the Son, Second Hypostasis (hypothesis of immobility), who confirms Life (= God) in his visible manifestation called the Creation, is eternally born.

He is the One thanks to whom all the things that exist are in existence, and without him nothing that is would be.

It is because he is, that he calls God (= Life) his Father. But the Father would not be, without the Son.

If the Will to Die were as powerful as the Will to Live, the Son would not be, nor the Father, nor the Creation.

Consequently, the Son is the Victory of the Father.

But Satan (= Negation of Life) is immortal, the same as the Father, the same as the Son.

Eternally, the struggle between Life and Death goes on.

That is why, at the very instant when the Son is born, the Negator invites him to die.

The struggle, which was, is, and will eternally be within the First Hypostasis (hypothesis of immobility), immediately repeats in the Second. The morning triumph lasts only an instant.

Adversary of the Father (God = Life), Satan is that also of the Son. He struggles against the latter, as he struggles against the former.

But just as the Father triumphs eternally in giving birth to the Son, the Son triumphs eternally in emanating the Third Hypostasis (hypothesis of immobility): the Wholesome Spirit, or Holy Spirit who reconfirms the existence of the visible world.

It is that One of whom it is said in the Christian Credo: "I believe in the Holy Spirit, the Lord who maintains Life; who emanates from the Father and the Son, and triumphs with them in the Heavens, eternally."*

But the Woman, to whom Satan has confided his secret, will prove to you—if you find her!—that the Holy Spirit, or Wholesome Spirit, is, in the Triangle formed by the Three Hypostases (the three successive hypotheses of immobility), feminine in essence . . .

Here is placed the second formidable secret of the Royal Art, and to understand it, it is necessary that you meditate at length on the following teaching:

In the purity of unreal abstraction, in the ice of Nothingness where the lonely duel of the Yes and the No takes place, it is not a question of sexes, but neither is it a question of God (= Life), because unreal abstraction does not conceive of Life.

But unreal abstraction has never been. Man imagines it because his Reason belongs to Satan (= the Will to Die).

Man must dream this proud Satanic purity, because without it he would not struggle against God (= Life), and the world, then, would not be. We have said it.

If Man were alone, without Woman, and composed only of the Heart, which presides over Balance, and Reason, which tends toward nullity, none of the things that make up the Universe could maintain themselves.

Having given its name to each animal, to each plant, to each

---

*This is similar to all versions of the Nicene Creed, but it does not exactly match any version with which I am familiar.

element, Adam would have destroyed the world if, in the Night that followed the Day of the Word, God (= Life) had not removed one of his ribs to oppose the Woman to him: Eve!

The appearance of Eve near Adam in the biblical Paradise symbolizes the second Victory, eternal like the first (the birth of the Son), of God = Life. It is the Victory of the Son.

You can imagine, O disciple, the eternal birth of the Son of God outside of the reality of the manifested world.

You can believe—imagine, if you know it—in the abstract Victory of the Yes over the No (the birth of the Son), without there being any need for your Reason to conceive of the visible Universe.

But you will not imagine—for your Reason itself refutes it—the possibility of a confirmation of the Will to Live in the visible world (= God) if that world did not exist.

The second Victory of God (= Life), the Wholesome Spirit or the Holy Spirit, is inconceivable in abstraction.

It is also inconceivable, in its crystalline purity, everywhere that Balance reigns (= the Heart that accepts all the drops of blood, without any distinction), and everywhere that Reason (= Satan) rages. For where the No is mixed in, the Yes is not alone.

O disciple! The Wholesome Spirit (Yes, Yes) or the Holy Spirit is found in the Feminine, which is beyond the Heart, beyond Justice, beyond Balance, and opposite of Reason.

The Heart, in your body, symbolizes the first Victory of Life. But the pure Feminine, Intelligence without Learning, opposed to your pure Masculine (Reason), is the second Victory of God (= Life). It is the confirmation of Life in the visible world by direct Intelligence without the analysis of Doubt.

If the Woman, the pure virgin, had been able to triumph in conformity with the hopes of certain Gnostic schools, Satan would have disappeared, because the Reason of the Man would then have been vanquished. It would have been the definitive triumph of God (= Life), and the Man, prostrate before the adored, but *respected,* Woman would have celebrated the end of the world. For with the No no longer in existence, the Yes would have ceased.

That is why, O disciple, the morning smile does not last more than an instant.

And now meditate upon this:

When God (= Life) opposed to Adam, in the biblical Paradise, the immaculate spouse, the virgin Eve, and when the Bridegroom found her beautiful, Satan took the form of a Serpent (symbol of wisdom) and murmured into the ear of the Woman:

"O Eve, splendid creature! Why has God, the Lord of Life, forbidden you to offer yourself to the Man, your husband? Why must Adam content himself with admiring your beauty, without biting into the fruit hidden in your charming forest? Isn't it an injustice to condemn you to eternal sterility and deprive you of the best of the fruits of this garden?"

Then Eve answered:

"The Lord of Life has permitted the Man, my husband, and

me, his wife, to feed ourselves from all the fruits that decorate and cheer this garden, but he has said that the fruit hidden in my forest was the fruit of Death."

But Satan, wrapping the Woman in his serpentine caress, murmured this to her:

"O Eve! Adorable Woman! The Lord of Life deceives himself and deceives you. For that I reproach him Day and Night. What he calls the 'fruit of Death' grants, on the contrary, immortality, science, and omnipotence to him who nourishes himself from it. It is undoubtedly to keep your husband in his state of slavery that he has hidden the best of you in your depths."

And, slipping through the warm moss of the troubled beauty, Satan deposited there his acid venom.

Eve knew the first shudder of love, and revealed the secret of it to Adam.

The Serpent, Satan, the Will to Die, these Three that are only one, taught voluptuousness to the Woman, who from that time became the Lover who attracts the Man to his Woman not for the Victory of Life (= God), but for the Victory of Death (= Satan), and Eve, that Second Triumph, that living symbol of the Third Hypostasis, in which Intelligence replaces Reason, became the arena of the struggle between Life and Death.

Satan introduced the Will to Die where there had only been the Will to Live!

Make no mistake about what we are teaching you here, O disciple, and note well that in the beginning the Woman was without Reason, which in the Man only opposed human to Divine, the Satanic spirit of the will toward liberation by domination of the visible world, to the Divine Spirit of the Will to Live in eternal harmony with God (= Life). The Man only knew the name of everything, every plant, every animal.

In the beginning the two Hearts—that of the Man and that of the Woman—being in perfect Balance, and sex not yet having spoken, only the head of Eve opposed the head of Adam, and the charming smile of her lips and of her eyes chased away the boredom of the Man, who felt lost in the middle of the silence of the animals whose names he knew too well.

In that brief paradisiacal period, on that Second Morning of the Divine Triangle, Satan was vanquished and God (= Life) triumphed.

But after the sin, the voluptuous Fall of Adam and Eve, the struggle of the Day and the Night recommenced.

Since that time this struggle has been within the human couple. The head of the Man belongs to Satan (–), the head of the Woman to God (+), the sex of the Woman to Satan (–), the sex of the Man to God (+).

That is why the sin committed by the first couple involved cerebral punishment for the Man ("Thou shalt gain thy bread by the sweat of thy brow"), and punishment of the womb for the Woman ("In pain shalt thou give birth").

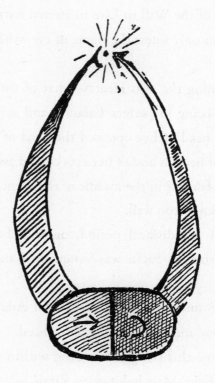

The Couple

But the very thing that was a fault can become, must become, redemption.*[1]

It is said: "The Woman will crush the head of the Serpent and give back to the visible world the Son of God, the Son of Man, who will chase Death away from Life."†[2]

It is also said: "I will separate the Woman from the Serpent, and I will put hatred between the two."

The Woman who will vanquish Satan within her womb, that one will regenerate the world, for "just as Death entered into everyone and everything through one who was following the Woman, it will be withdrawn from everyone and everything thanks to the Victory of One, through the Woman."

---

*This is not, in itself, a new idea. It was put into practice very dramatically by the Gnostic followers of Carpocrates in the early Christian centuries. More outspoken (and less prudish) ancient writers tell us that the Carpocratians made sex part of their worship service, choosing an attractive young man and woman to make love in front of the congregation. This act was considered holy and they did not find it shocking. In fact, when the service was over they would file past the place where the couple had lain, and each person would dip a finger into the residual semen there and take it as a form of communion. Some say that Naglowska did something similar, but I have found no proof of it. It may, however, be hinted at: "The high priestess, announcer of the new Term, will signal the beginning and the end of the rite to the Assembly, and through her will be poured out upon the congregation the Divine Energy liberated through the contact of the bodies in the Sanctuary. The men and women who will make up this congregation will derive therefrom great moral and spiritual well-being and their own vital energy will be fortified and sanctified thereby."—"La Flèche" (a pseudonym of Maria de Naglowska).

†This idea that it is the Woman herself who will crush the head of the Serpent, rather than a male among her progeny, is distinctly Western, having come from the Latin of Saint Jerome's Vulgate translation. Since this is supported neither by the Masoretic Hebrew text nor by the Greek of the Septuagint (LXX, which is the basis of the Old Testament in use in the Orthodox Church), it is likely that Naglowska picked this idea up in Europe rather than in Russia.

And since that day, since the day of the Origin (which never was!), the feminine sex has been searching through all women to find the Way to vanquish Satan. Attempt after attempt, the generations pass.

O disciple! Today the Woman has found the Way.* The key of the Great Secret has been unveiled to Her who has been able to reject the malefic gift of Reason in order to let shine in Her only the pure Light of Intelligence.

If you encounter Her, She will prove to you what you do not know.

For you must not accept anything without palpable proof. It is to this that you have been condemned.

*To vanquish Satan.

THE CALVARY
OF REASON

They will be two to be complete, but they will not
understand each other because they are not perfect.

HANOUM[*1]

We have told you, O disciple, that you will first climb the Calvary of Reason.

We have told you that no Initiate can serve God if he has not first served Satan[†] until he reaches the Summit.

If you have understood the teachings contained in the chapters that precede this one entitled "The Calvary of Reason," we can tell you more.

Listen well, and do not be an idolater.[‡]

---

[*]Hanoum, or F. Hanoum, is another pseudonym of Maria de Naglowska. I say this in spite of the imaginary personal descriptions given in "Une Séance Magique," *La Flèche Organe d'Action Magique.*
[†]Naglowska has already said that Satan = Reason, presumably the interpretation here.
[‡]This is shorthand for "Do not imagine Satan as living outside of yourself."

As shown by the symbol you have just seen (p. 42) and upon which we invite you to meditate at length, the man in whom Reason is not very strong is neither White nor Black. He is gray. In him the Heart is dominant, the Heart that accepts all the drops of blood without distinction.

Such a man belongs to the crowd, and like the crowd, he likes or he detests, but he never reasons.

To such a man (and there are legions!) nothing can be said, because he discerns nothing. One can touch his Heart, then he blindly obeys, for it seems to him that one is offering him what he wants. One can shock him, then he becomes irritated, for it seems to him that one wishes to impose upon him something that he does not like.

Essentially, such a man—the man of the crowd—does not differ from the ordinary woman, from her whom we have called blind. Like her, he neither serves Satan (the Negation of Life) nor God (the Affirmation of Life) in particular.

He is the unconscious arena of the eternal struggle of the Yes and the No, the same as animals, the same as plants.

And he is incoherent and harmonious at the same time, like everything that makes up the Universe.

It is in this sense that he obeys God (to obey is not to serve!), for in not accentuating either the White or the Black, he flows, like all the drops that compose the human flood, toward the Ocean of which he is unaware.

And we have said since the beginning of this book that every human river must stay in its channel.

It must, because in order that the Universal Angle should re-form itself at the predetermined instant, contributing thus to the eternal re-formation of the Triangle, it is necessary that the whole human stream (except for the inevitable losses) should bend upon itself at the same instant, at the same epoch.

It is necessary, because such is the Will of the Stronger, the Will of God (= Life). It will not be of any use to you to oppose yourself to the Law of the Stronger.

But the same Law, which wishes that, wishes also that there should be a lever at the morning hour of Awakening.

The Initiates form this lever. That is why Initiates are necessary.

If it were not necessary, we would not have received the order to write this book. For what we unveil here is not for the crowd, but only for the elect, for those adult persons who deserve to know where they come from and where they are going.

Are you one of them, you, O disciple, who are stirred by these things? Examine your conscience. Do you belong to those who, tired of belonging to the mediocre crowd of the profane, start out resolutely upon dangerous paths?

You will not know in advance where the goal is, but you will be told right away that up there Hanging awaits you, for the rose blossoms so that its seed may fall.

Do you feel in yourself this mad devotion?

The instant of your resolution belongs to you; the rest belongs to God (Yes—No—Yes).

If, on the other hand, you are deceiving yourself, if your courage is nothing more than vanity, sleep will take you again and you will be, in the crowd, a profane malcontent.

But may your will be done! Listen well.

When an adult person, worthy of knowing where he comes from and where he is going, recognizes that the gray crowd is like a wild forest with no way out, he is seized by fear and cries out, as Dante did, "I've lost my way!"

> *Nel mezzo del cammin di nostra vita*
> *M'incontrai per una selva oscura*
> *Chè la diritta via era smarrita*

From that time on he finds himself opposed to the wild forest, the gray crowd, and naturally he revolts against God (= Life). He then asks his mother, "Why have you given me birth?"

Having said that, he finds himself outside the vicious circle of habitual life, where the Yes and the No are mingled in the contradictory harmony of the Continuance, protected by the shield of the Law, and in him the No gets the upper hand.

Satan* then takes possession of his vital force, subjects it to his own negative power, and lights within the rebel Man the formidable Fire of the Black Gold.

This Fire burns everything and spreads an odor of sulfur. It is the basis of the magic by means of which the Man, freed from the chains of the crowd, works Good or Evil at will.

---

*The Negator of Life within us.

The Satanic Fire burns in the head of the Man, which then absorbs all the forces distributed throughout his body and more particularly those within his sex.

All the Sun stored up in the winged rod of the Man then converges on the top of his head, and if God (= Life = Yes) abandoned him, soon the Freedman would be no more, or would only be to the extent that he would become a perfect localization of Satan (= No).

This is certainly what the Spirit of Evil, the Spirit of Negation, has been seeking for as long as the world has been world.

But equally since the world has been world, the Yes has been combating the No: everywhere, in a general fashion, and in particular where the No predominates.

Seeing that the Man, freed from the chains of the crowd, has started upon the dangerous paths of the initiatic Mountain, Life (= God) hurries before him and bars the passage.

Then, from the wild forest, symbolical animals run up and tempt the Initiate . . . Disciple, you who wish to listen to us, learn this: "temptations" come from God and not from Satan.

Have you seen, in Egypt (land of initiatic suffering), the four elements that compose the Sphinx: the Charger, the Lion, the Eagle, and the Woman? Have your professors given you the key to this wise composition? Have they told you that these four, which separately symbolize the four great successive tests to which one submitted the "candidates" in that distant time of the mysteries of Isis, together are the chant of the Call to Order of Life (= God)?

Have you understood that the Man who is carried away by the

influence of Satan has no need of tests to arrive at the Summit? The Will of the No is straight like that of the Yes, but it is the struggle between the two that makes the ways tortuous. At each stage—Charger,* Lion, Eagle, Woman—you again become the arena, and two Masters fight within you. But you are a living arena, and you can, if you wish, favor one or the other of the two combatants.

If you straddle the Charger and bend it to your orders, Satan is victorious in you and God (= Life) vanquished.

If you subdue the Lion and escape from its claws, it is still Satan that rejoices.

If, like the Eagle, you rise to the Heavens and fix with your eyes the dazzling face of the Sun, it is the No that triumphs in you, for then you have seen Life (= God), and you have made yourself equal to the Her, the Woman, which God opposes to you in order that the Universe should continue.

In the initiatic schools, which keep "the Tradition" in the troubled epochs of the Night of Time, such as the one in which we are living at this moment, the forms subsist, but the sense has been lost.

That is why one no longer knows where Satan is, where God is, where life intermixed of these two is.

One no longer knows what purity is, and above all, one no longer knows why it is needed.

---

*In Naglowska's symbolism, the White Charger always represents sexual energy. As she pointed out, it is a vehicle that can take one far, but it must be controlled and properly directed.

The Triumph of Reason

Now, by the light of our teachings, anxious disciple, you are beginning to see clearly.

You are beginning to understand that in order to be able to help God (= Life) to re-form at Midnight—and it is now Midnight—the Angle of Salvation, the Angle that bends the human river upon itself, making it form the Eternal Triangle, you must first follow Satan upon the paths of his Calvary. You must acquire the Black Purity, intensifying it unceasingly until the Lunar Crescent is formed on your forehead.

The great Moses did as much and, on Mount Sinai, two horns formed above his forehead: the Moon of Acceptance.

We will speak to you later of this mystery, which explains the Rite of Hanging (twelfth arcanum of the Tarot), but for now concentrate your attention on the first of the Four Tests, the Test of the Charger.

THE WHITE
CHARGER

*You will loathe your flesh and you will scorn it until
the day when, vanquished, you will know my Truth.*

LA FLÈCHE[*1]

I f you straddle the Charger[†] and bend it to your orders, Satan is
victorious in you and God (= Life) vanquished.

O disciple! Do not go into combat if your defensive weapon, the
shield (= your body), is not solid.

Do not climb the initiatic Mountain, do not seek the apple that
grants the Knowledge of Good and Evil, if your heart, your liver,
your kidneys, your stomach, and your intestines are not in perfect
Balance and functioning according to the formal Law of Life: Yes,
No, Yes, No, Yes, No continually.

---

*I maintain that "La Flèche" is also a pseudonym of Maria de Naglowska, in spite
of the imaginary personal descriptions in "Une Séance Magique," *La Flèche Organe
d'Action Magique.*
†The White Charger represents sexual energy.

The Ascension of the arid slope is not a pleasure party. It is a priesthood, and "We do not need the weak, the disordered, the unhealthy and preoccupied, the debauched, extreme fornicators, babblers, thieves, gluttons, men for whom nothing is healthy. We want," so speak the Yes and the No, as they descend into the human arena, "a solid and even ground."

The preparation of this soil is the work of the Sweeper, and he will remain in the Court as long as he has not learned to be silent, to respect the moral and physical good of others, to master his various appetites, to patiently await his turn to speak and to act.

No man can do this work in an efficacious fashion if he is not subject to a Master who guides his steps. That is why every Sweeper shall give his word of obedience to the Superior put in charge of his instruction.

Nota bene: In a well-organized initiatic association, there is no unworthy Superior.

"It is because you have forgotten that," say the Lords of the Yes and the No, "that your temples are no longer what they originally were."

But you will build a new Temple for a new initiation.

Now, when the Superior in charge of your instruction has declared that your preparation is sufficient, he will bring you before the Warriors, and the Assembly of these venerable ones will ask you thrice the following question:

"Younger Brother, are your feet and your hands well washed?"

And you will thrice respond, "Yes," if in the course of the period of preparation you have well understood that the dust that hindered your acts, from the time when you worked in the courtyard, was white.

The Speaker of the Assembly will then say to you:

"Younger Brother, you are deceiving yourself, for it is true that your hands are washed and your body well balanced, as your Brother Superior declares, whose word may not be doubted because he knows the responsibility incumbent upon him in case of a mistake regarding you; your feet, however, are not washed, because you are still profaning your legs. Younger Brother, you have not yet straddled the White Charger, whose wild gallop is free in you."

And if truly you have well understood why you were sweeping in the Court, when night was falling and the Freedmen were entering into the Temple to light the Tapers and sing the canticles of glory before the Eternal Triangle, you will proudly answer:

"He who walks in the dust has his feet soiled, obviously. But I shall subdue the Charger if you put me to the test, for my hands are washed, as you recognize, and my body solid, as you are aware. Test me!"

If the Venerable Warriors recognize that in your answer there does not breathe a vain pride, but rather a justified boldness, they will put you to the test.

You will be admitted, after a short period of special preparation, to a test session held for you.

The Superior in charge of your instruction will take you into the hall of ablutions, and you will wash yourself carefully from head to foot.

You will again put on the short red tunic of natural silk, which symbolizes the blood of your arteries, the blood, which is the basis of your strength and the main reason for your admission into the Court of the Confraternity.

For it will be written in your Statutes: "The anemic man shall not enter this enclosure, and let him not complain, for our goal is to conquer the Sun. And can one vanquish the Divine Star if one does not carry its essence within himself?

While wrapping your body in the red tunic, you will say the following out loud:

"At my entry into the Court of the Confraternity of the Knights of the Golden Arrow, I did not see my blood except when I wounded myself. I will now wear its color upon my skin, for I no longer fear the Bull, which this Light excites. In sweeping the Court, I have tamed the beast."

Your Superior will then perfume you with the fragrant essence that is propitious for you, and you will follow him, barefoot, into the reception hall of the Second Degree.

You will stop in front of the closed door and your Guide will knock, demanding that it be opened to you.

The Guardian of the Door will answer from the inside of the hall: "Who comes? Who knocks at the door that is closed to the profane?" And your Guide will say: "A Man who has cleaned his courtyard and who comes here for his recompense." "What is the name of this Man, and what is his color?" "He is called the Detached-from-the-Tree, and his tunic is red," your Guide will say.

"Let he himself knock at the closed door!" the Guardian of the Temple will cry out. "Here one does not open. If he is powerful, let him enter."

And you will struggle then against the closed door, and you will enter if you break it.

When your strength has conquered the obstacle of the wood, the Guardian will still oppose himself to your entry, barring the passage with his two arms.

"You have broken the inert wood!" he will cry out. "Now try to push away this living barrier."

And if your muscles are solid and your resolution firm, you will push away the Guardian, and you will enter into the hall.

Then the Freedmen and the Venerable Warriors will receive you with joy, to the sound of horns and trumpets.

But while the tumult is great and before you have caught your breath, the Guardian will rush upon you and throw over your head a black hooded robe with the visor lowered.

You will be plunged into deep Night and you will hear the thundering voice of the Guardian, who will utter this word: "It is forbidden that a blind person should see this Assembly."

Your Guide will immediately take up your defense, saying this: "This Man is not blind, I have given him sight." "Let him prove it!" the Guardian will shout.

Then each one will take his place and, staying in the middle of the hall, you will undergo the interrogatory of admission to the Second Degree of the Satanic* Initiation of the Knights of the Golden Arrow.

---

*It is called Satanic because, in standing for the No and controlling the sexual energy (for such is the nature of the test), it is opposing, or resisting, Life.

By your answers to the questions that are posed to you and which you will not know in advance, you will have to prove that you have understood why the Mountain that you wish to climb is black* and why, henceforth, you must be odious to the crowds.

For it shall be written in your books of study:

"Because he has left them, seeking new paths and other shores, vulgar men and women have placed him on the index.

"The men and women of the crowd are right, and so is he, for those who belong to the Earth must defend what is of the Earth—the contradictory harmony of the Eternal Continuance—but the Freedmen of obedience to the Court of the Knights of the Golden Arrow must combat this Savagery without fear of Death:

"In themselves first of all, then in their Younger Brothers and peers, and thirdly in all of humanity.

"You shall combat within yourselves the Savagery (= the incoherent harmony of the Continuance), in mastering your emotions of every kind: the emotions arising from the Vision of new things. At every instant you will be interiorly cold, but exteriorly you will play your role in the Human Comedy to perfection, conforming exactly to the 'Code of the Jester' taught to you in the Court.

---

*The Mountain is black because that color represents the No of sexual control. The candidate, having adopted higher standards for himself, thereby becomes odious to the crowds, who tend to require homogeneity.

The Light of Sex

"Always kind, you will be indifferent with regard to all. You will not prefer anyone, you will not love anyone, for to love is to attract into yourself the fluidic image of another. Now, in attracting into yourself the image of a profane man or woman, you destroy the work of black* purification that you have undertaken here, and it is written: 'He who wishes to come to Me must leave his father, his mother, his brothers and sisters, his children and his outside friends.' The Freedman of obedience to the Court of the Knights of the Golden Arrow has no brothers elsewhere than here."

This passage from the book of study entitled "Satanic† Ethics" will be read to you by a Freedman of the Court after the interrogatory, and at the end of this reading you will say: "I have no other brothers but those whose Candles are lighted here."

"Have you seen these Candles?" they will ask you.

And you will answer: "In the dark hours of the Twilight of Time, when I was working in the Court that was covered with white dust, some Black Shadows‡ passed. The Superior who presided over my work of purification would say to me, 'Look at those men! They have conquered the Blood and the Water, and now they are going into the Temple to maintain the light of their Candles.'

---

*Again, black represents the No of sexual control, which resists unregulated Life.
†It should be obvious by now that Satan, as anything outside of ourselves, has nothing to do with it.
‡These are his Elder Brothers in the Order.

And my Guide added, 'your time will come, be patient.' Now, my time has arrived, I want to light my Candle."

And you will believe, in your naïveté, that the Candle is made of wax and that one lights it with a match. But it will be with you as it was with the Freedman whose testimony, kept in our archives, we now present.

THE TRUE TESTIMONY OF A FREE HUNTER OF THE COURT OF THE KNIGHTS OF THE GOLDEN ARROW

I had claimed my right to light my Candle, for no objection had been made by the Venerable Warriors and the Freedmen of the Court of the Knights of the Golden Arrow after the very precise answers I had given in the course of my interrogatory.

It is true that under the hooded robe with the visor lowered I could not tell whether these Sirs looked upon me approvingly or critically.

Their questions and my answers are summarized approximately as follows:

"Provisional guest of the Temple of the Arrow, from where do you come?"

"I come from the Court of Obedience of the Knights of the Golden Arrow."

"What did you do in this Court?"

"I swept from myself the white dust that hindered my movements and my acts in the profane fray."

"Of what color are you now?"

"I am red, for my blood is pure and my senses mastered."

"What is your intention?"

"I wish to climb the black slope, in order to receive the Sun in my eyes. I wish to conquer Water and Air, in order to deserve the Test of Fire."

I waited for further questions, for it seemed to me that my examiners should realize exactly what were my ideas of Water, Air, and the Victory of these two powerful Resistances of the Affirmation of Life (= God), but there was nothing more, or at least not right away, and certainly not in the manner that I supposed.

There must have been, after my last answer noted above, a prolonged silence, and in the deep Night where I found myself it was impossible for me to guess whether anything was going on around me.

All of a sudden a particularly strong voice struck my ear with this question:

"Candidate for the Corps of the Freedmen, what is your emblem?"

Without an instant for reflection I cried out, "NO is my emblem."

Then the trumpets and the hunting horns played a triumphant Warrior tune, which seemed to multiply in the air the Negation that I had proclaimed.

Someone then proposed to free me from the hooded robe, pretending that my "sight" was proven and my right to see the Assembly acquired, but one of the Warriors, the Chief, no doubt, opposed it and ordered the reading of the passage in the book of study entitled "Satanic Ethics," which ends with the sentence, "The Freedman of obedience to the Court of the Knights of the Golden Arrow has no brothers elsewhere than here."

I was and I am deeply convinced of the absolute necessity of this hard ethic, in view of the final Victory; that is why, to the question that was put to me, "Candidate for the Corps of the Freedmen, do you accept these principles?" I answered resolutely, "Yes, and henceforth I shall have no other brothers but those whose Candles are lighted here. I claim the right to light mine in my turn."

Then a strange thing happened, one that I was truly not expecting. My hooded robe was removed, very slowly, by means of a hook that carried it into the depths of the Cone overhanging the hall of receptions of the Confraternity of the Knights of the Golden Arrow. My liberation from Night began at the legs, and while I was feeling a mild air current gliding between my two thighs, the raising of the hooded cloak was interrupted for an instant at the height of my male organ.

Then the machinery moving the hook was reactivated, and the hooded robe rose up to my neck.

Here the pause was long, and a stringed instrument, perhaps a violin, played a soft melody during the halt, full of nostalgic regret. I seemed to hear a distant voice that sorrowfully sobbed.

My head was freed at one swoop, when this sublime voice was drowned in the metallic chords of the trumpets and the horns resuming their martial accents.

It was deafening.

I suddenly felt dizzy, because of the sudden light, the bewildering music, and the strange odor that filled the atmosphere. It was a very pronounced male odor, mixed with other more subtle aromas.

The dizziness having passed, I saw some men forming a circle around me. I had time to notice their virile nudity, though they were already crossing their broad capes of black silk with a rapid motion.

I saw that the high walls of the round hall were hung with black and decorated with symbolic red and gold designs. The electric lights were numerous. In front of me, in two wings each having two superimposed rows, sat the Venerable Warriors, dressed in black with gold brocade, and the Freedmen of the Court, in hunting clothes.

The deep shadows of the Cone, which overhung the hall with its heavy Night, contained an infinitely attractive mystery. One could barely distinguish there the shining of a light like that of a star.

They allowed me a few minutes to see all that.

Then, undoubtedly deciding that I had seen enough, one of the Warriors—the Chief, no doubt—descended the stairs of the narrow staircase that had been contrived between the two wings of the tribunal, matching his steps to the rhythm of the military music played by an orchestra that I did not see. He approached the living circle that surrounded me.

Meanwhile, I had realized that the men who formed this circle numbered ten.

The Chief drew his shining sword, which a trick of the light had tinted with red, and cut the symbolic circle with a superb gesture.

Then the men wrapped in black silk went to the right and the left, like the wings of a big bird, and arranged themselves in a straight line behind me.

The music softened its accents.

The Chief turned toward the Assembly of the Warriors and Hunters and said in a strong voice:

"My Lords the Venerable Warriors, and Free Hunters of the Court of the Knights of the Golden Arrow, here is a new Man before you!"

At the same second the whole Assembly stood and, while the Warriors saluted me with their unsheathed swords, the Hunters sang in chorus the *Salute* of our Confraternity:

"Hail to you, O Younger Brother, born at this instant into the Male Light* of Satan! May his will be propitious to you!"

Very kindly, the Chief asked me to respond.

I held out my arms toward the Assembly, and I shouted Out with all my strength:

"Hail to you, Older Brothers, Venerable Warriors and free Hunters! May my effort joined to yours be efficacious for the Common Cause!"

"May the No triumph!" the Warriors shouted with a single voice, brusquely flourishing their swords.

---

*The black Light of the No, representing sexual control (thus opposing Life).

I saw then twelve Lunar Crescents directed against me.

I looked at the Chief, and I noticed that the hilt of his sword had the same form.

Seeing my realization, the Chief smiled agreeably.

"My Lords the Hunters!" he cried out, "Come to receive this Young Brother into your Corps of Freedmen."

Immediately the procession formed, and the Hunters of the Court of the Knights of the Golden Arrow descended single file into the arena where I found myself and arranged themselves on each side in perpendicular lines with respect to the men wrapped in black silk.

With a rhythmic and well-coordinated movement, they took off their belts and their black jackets, which they threw to the ground behind them, and appeared to my dazzled eyes in tight red leotards with the striking Satanic emblem "NO" artfully embroidered on the chest.

The Hunters were twelve in number, so there must have been six on each side.

The Chief gave me then the iron benediction: with the point of his sword he touched one after the other my nervous centers ruling the Sex, the Heart, and the Brain, then, with a light touch, he traced on my body the reversed Triangle: from the right armpit to the left armpit, and from there to the male organ, and from the latter again to the right armpit.

He then drew back a step, raised his palms toward the Star that scintillated in the depths of the Black Cone, and said in a voice full of mystical conviction:

"Star of the Morning, O You who announce the Awakening after the Dark Night, guide the movements and the acts of this young Freedman, who will go away now to hunt the Lion in the wild forest of humanity. Guide his steps in the terrible Test of the Water and bring him back here victorious. This evening he will light his votive lamp in the Temple, by means of his sacred Taper. I beg of you, in the name of all of my Brothers gathered here and dispersed throughout the world, receive his lamp for good effect. For, O Star of the Morning, blue and pure, what would you do without us?"

"Present!" shouted the men gathered in the hall, myself included.

That made in all thirty-six male voices.

THE INITIATIC BANQUET AND THE VIRILE TAPER

The true testimony of the Free Hunter of the Court of the Knights of the Golden Arrow continues thus:

My Older Brothers, the Free Hunters of the Court of Obedience of the Knights of the Golden Arrow, helped me put on the uniform of the Second Degree of Satanic* Initiation, which is composed as follows: first the tight leotard of red silk, put together in such a way as to cover the whole body except for the head and the hands, then the short pants and the jacket of black cloth, molding the body down to the knees. The jacket is held in at the waist by a leather belt, and high, polished boots protect the feet and the calves over the red silk of the leotard.

---

*It is only Satanic in the sense that it represents the No of sexual control, which is what the ritual is about.

The Brothers also gave me black riding gloves lined with white,* which I stuck into my belt, and a large felt hat decorated with a peacock feather, which I kept in my hand.

The Satanic emblem, No, was only embroidered, in black letters, on the leotard and at the bottom of the red lining of the hat. One did not see it at all when the jacket was buttoned and the head covered.

I was not to receive until later, after the banquet and the Candle ceremony, the symbolic bow and the quiver with the golden arrows of our Hunters, for, since the test was not over, I remained a junior in the midst of these bold Hunters.

When I was dressed, the Hunters, my Brothers, put on their jackets, their belts, their bows, and their quivers held at the shoulder by a golden cord, and the Chief invited the Venerable Warriors to descend into the arena. Single file, these Sirs came down the narrow steps, and, approaching me one by one, they gave me the fraternal embrace.

The Hunters followed their example, and the Chief embraced me last, after the ten witnesses enveloped in black silk.

I thus received, the day of my reception into the Corps of the Freedmen of the Court of Obedience of the Knights of the Golden Arrow, seventy† male kisses.

We sang, after that, the prayers that we learn in our study books.

---

*The black gloves lined with white symbolize the necessity for both the Yes and the No, and their Balance, in our actions.

†(35 × 2)

It was midnight when the Chief called a respite for the banquet.

Then the floor-well opened up in the middle of the arena, and a large round table, surrounded by thirty-six carved-wood stools, came up out of the basement, covered for the meal and loaded with various plates and viands.

"Let the supper begin, in a lively mood!" the Chief called out, seating himself at the table.

We each occupied our place, which we knew by the label attached to the candelabra placed before each covered plate. The labels carried the name and age* of each guest, and each candelabra had thirteen Candles. When everyone was seated, one of the Warriors—and I recognized him as the Guardian who had opposed my entry into the Temple at the beginning of the session—went around the table presenting to the Warriors and Hunters, on a small golden plate, a votive lamp and a small wax Candle. By means of this Candle, the guests lit the Tapers of their candelabras, bringing to them the fire taken from the lamp. The Hunters lit only the Candles of the lower row, which contained seven, and each lit only the number corresponding to the figure of his age counted from the moment of his Rebirth in the Temple of the Confraternity. The Warriors lit the whole lower row and as many of the five Candles of the upper row as the grades they had acquired within the Initiation of the Third Degree. Only the Chief lit all thirteen Candles.

The Guardian of the Temple did not present the lamp with the Sacred Fire to me, because my Virile Taper had not been ritually lit.

---

*The number of years in the Order.

This would not take place until about two o'clock in the morning.

They extinguished the electric lamps, and the meal commenced.

The black shadow, which surrounded us on all sides, totally hid the decorated walls and galleries. Only the Star,* in the depths of the Cone† that overhung the hall, broke the darkness above our heads.

The round table, illuminated by the two hundred eighty-three Candles of our candelabras, was like a luminous island in the midst of the night.

We served ourselves, each according to his appetite and without shyness. Rare meats were in abundance, as were richly seasoned salads. Fruits from Spain and Italy filled the large wicker baskets, and the wines of France were of the best vintages. As we ate, we chatted gaily.

But, toward the end of the meal, the conversation became more serious. Several Venerable Warriors expressed their concern with regard to the lamentable political situation in all the countries of Europe, and the Free Hunters quieted down to listen attentively. For, evidently, the members of the Confraternity of the Knights of the Golden Arrow could not remain indifferent in the face of what was happening outside.

When the Brothers, Venerable Warriors, had exchanged their opinions, the Chief, who, seemingly plunged into deep reflection,

---

*This Star is always symbolic of the Morning Star that will usher in the New Era of the Third Term.

†The Cone appears to symbolize the higher planes. Naglowska occasionally appended the phrase "by order of the Cone" to certain of her writings.

had remained silent until then, made us the following speech:

"What characterizes the Dark Epoch through which we are passing is the fall of the crowns, unworthily usurped. Peoples revolt and massacre the false shepherds. It is only Justice, and we do not need to deplore this natural reaction of elementary forces distributed throughout the crowds. Suffering comes of it, it is true, but that is still just, because every disorder deserves its punishment, its pain, arising from the lost equilibrium.

"As to what concerns us, we are not there to take pity, nor to mitigate misery; others besides us fill this need according to the measure of their strength. We are the Black Confraternity, whose only role consists in receiving the Morning Star and directing the rays through the New Humanity.

"Let us not waste our strength on sterile acts. The Morning is near and the Star has need of all of us. Our public work will soon begin.

"We will then come out of the shadow in which we have hidden ourselves during those long centuries, and we shall openly proclaim the Truth of the Wholesome Satanic* Doctrine. This, not to invite the crowds to follow our example, or to stupidly copy our attitudes, but to inculcate in them the truths that belong to them and to habituate them to respect those that are not for everyone.

"For that is the sickness of the century: each believes himself capable of everything and each imagines that all privileges are due to him.

"Now, privileges are acquired at the cost of a great effort. It is an

---

*Remember: Do not be an idolater.

essential point that we must prove to the masses, for them to listen to us.

"Another very important task will be to show that the Art Royal and the sciences and applied arts that derive from it should not be impoverished by making their profanation easy for the crowds, but that on the contrary the latter should raise themselves with a real effort, in order to make themselves worthy. To invite them to make the effort—there you have our task. We shall place the Apple of Knowledge very high, to make it difficult to pick. Only thus will the hierarchy of values be able to be reestablished and the current injustice brought to a halt."

The Chief fell silent, and then began again:

"Certainly, suffering humanity is not to blame, and its delirium does not come from itself. Those to blame are the initiated Knights who first permitted necessary pride to become unfeeling arrogance. The sickness entered into the century on the day that the rule of the round table was weakened by the elevation of the thrones.

"On that day, corruption began in the human hierarchy, and it propagated from rank to rank down to the Earth. Obligatory initiation was suppressed for sons of kings who inherited the power by simple birthright, which does not imply any effort toward Satanic purification. Lost in the white ignorance, profane kings made war on the Knights to please the Popes, whose victory thus became easy.

"But the Christ did not gain anything from it, for having lost the resistance of the Black Corps, his White Corps itself fell to pieces. It is this dust, O newly born Freedman, that you have swept in the Court, while we were here lighting our Virile Tapers. Your turn has come," the Chief added, fixing his piercing gaze upon me. "Clear off the table!"

The Venerable Warriors and the Free Knights of the Court of the Knights of the Golden Arrow became very serious. They all looked at me, and I read in their serious eyes this question: "Will he succeed?" The solemn instant approached.

Very quickly, the dishes and plates disappeared under the big round table, and the floor-well descended, taking the remains of the meal into the basement.

Each guest took his candelabra and placed it on the ground, at a distance of three steps beyond the periphery of the table, which was thus situated in the shadow separated from the night of the walls by the luminous circle of the two hundred eighty-three Candles burning with a Sacred Fire. I noticed that the Star, in the depths of the Cone, shone more strongly.

While the Venerable Warriors and the Free Hunters gathered in the shadow and the witnesses wrapped in black silk arranged themselves in a semicircle in the free space between the table and the Candles, the Chief pointed out to me my place: facing the witnesses and with back turned to the candelabra with the thirteen Candles lighted. It should be remembered that these thirteen Candles had been lit by the Chief. The latter and the Guide, who had instructed me when I was sweeping in the Court, placed themselves to my right and my left, at the two ends of the semicircle formed by the witnesses.

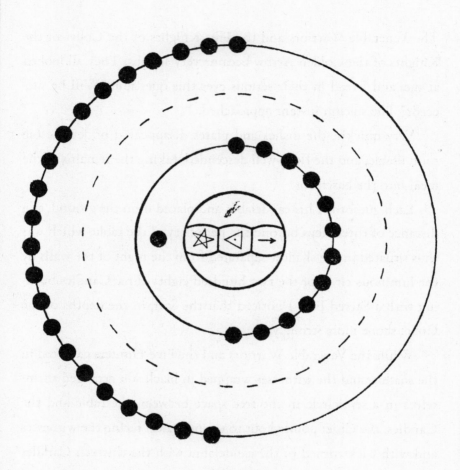

The Round Table

The Guardian of the Temple brought three large cushions, covered in white silk, and put them side by side on the round table. On the cushion that was placed closest to me, I saw a beautiful five-pointed star,* embroidered with gold thread. On the second cushion was detailed, also in gold, a regular Triangle whose apex was reversed[†] toward my direction. The design embroidered on the third cushion, still in gold, represented an arrow[‡] oriented toward the witnesses.

The most profound silence reigned in the Temple. With a ceremonious gesture, the Guardian invited the Venerable Warriors and the Free Hunters to come out of the shadow and to arrange themselves in a semicircle, facing that of the witnesses, but outside of the luminous circle formed by the candelabras. The attached picture shows the symbolical figure that was thus formed in the arena of the vast Satanic[§] Temple of the Knights of the Golden Arrow, where the most extraordinary thing that it had ever been given to me to see until that day was about to happen.

When each was in his place, immobile and concentrated, the Guardian of the Temple brought a strange, small apparatus, which he placed on the table near the outside edge of the third cushion, taking great care to turn it symmetrically in a perpendicular plane with reference to the arrow. The apparatus in question, which was located exactly in front of my navel, was composed of a sort of double-walled

---

*Symbol of the Morning Star.
†Symbol of the pubic triangle, itself symbolic of the Sacred Triangle.
‡Symbol of the epoch of the Third Term of the Trinity.
§See appendix B.

screen, of twenty-five square centimeters,* on a gilded base. They explained to me afterward how this apparatus had been prepared, but I do not have the right to reveal its secret for the moment, for I have sworn to wait *until the time is ripe and the starting signal has been given.* Meanwhile, I can say that between the two walls of the screen, which were both transparent, a delicate wick had been arranged, fixed upon a very small Candle.

The Venerable Warriors, the Free Hunters, and the witnesses, enveloped in black silk, were so deeply concentrated within themselves that it seemed that they saw nothing of these preparations. At the same time, while placing himself between the Chief and me, the Guardian of the Temple saluted with a ritual gesture first the witnesses, then the Venerable Warriors and the Free Hunters, and all these gentlemen bowed their heads deeply without, at the same time, bending the spine.

After that, the Guardian turned toward me and gave me a large salute with his two arms open. I answered as my Older Brothers had done. The Guardian then crossed the luminous circle in front of the semicircle formed by the Venerable Warriors and the Free Hunters, and exited this living enclosure at the opposite side, that is to say on my right.

With a slowly cadenced step he thrice went around the symbolic figure that we formed, and, having come back to the starting point at my right, outside the triple circle, he called out in his strong voice, "Let the Star descend!"

---

*Four square inches.

Immediately, all eyes were raised to the depths of the Cone where the blue light was growing more intense by the moment.

Suddenly, in the middle of this alluring light, a white cloud formed. It came down slowly, very slowly, right under the Star, and certainly would land upon the cushions.

I already guessed what this cloud was hiding, for I had understood many things when they were teaching me in the Court, but impatience to see the body promised for such a long time tormented me just the same, making the last few minutes very long.

It actually seemed to me that the descent of the Woman became even slower as the distance between her and the cushion diminished.

At last she was there, at the level of our heads, reposing in a hammock woven of silken cords and completely enveloped in a light and transparent fabric, blue and white, a splendid Woman of whom I could still only see the back and the buttocks.

I had difficulty repressing an agonized cry when I saw the Chief and my old Guide hold out their arms to receive her upon their crossed swords. It seemed to me that the steel was too hard for this charming flesh. But the Chief and the Guide softened the possible shock with their left arms, the Chief holding the nape of the neck and the Guide supporting the upper part of the thighs of the living statue, which they laid out respectfully on the soft little white bed formed by the three cushions.

The Woman slept a deep sleep, as it was to be according to the rule of the ritual, for this was the Water Test, the Test of the Flesh, and the Woman could not know what purpose she served for us.

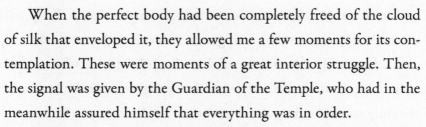

When the perfect body had been completely freed of the cloud of silk that enveloped it, they allowed me a few moments for its contemplation. These were moments of a great interior struggle. Then, the signal was given by the Guardian of the Temple, who had in the meanwhile assured himself that everything was in order.

Then, with a simultaneous movement, the Chief and my old Guide pressed, each on his side, an electrical button fixed to the edge of the round table in front of them. Immediately, a piece of the wood was released and glided down to the floor at my feet, bringing down with it in its fall the cushion upon which rested the legs of the beautiful Star. The latter were supported in time by the Chief and the Guide, who bent them and brought them back onto the second cushion.

I saw then two superb columns and the Doorway of Birth between them, the Doorway that everyone clears unawares when coming into the world.

The flesh invited me to redo the voyage in the reverse direction and with lucidity. The hour of the fearsome test had come, and the merciless witnesses were before me.

I cast to the ground my clothing of black and red like the fire that fears nothing; the implacable No engraved on my chest, I braved the danger.

A danger of Death, for I would have been blasted had I not succeeded. One wins or one loses everything in this test, which consists in straining one's vital will to the maximum of human capacity—superhuman!—and in lighting by the desired orgasm not the black cavern, but the luminous Summit of the Woman offered without awareness to this diabolical operation. The one being tested must remain dry to the end.

For it is written in our study books: "You will not permit your sacred force to be crystallized in mortal liquid."

I did what I had to do, and I succeeded, for at the exact instant calculated, the wick between the two walls of the screen lighted and thirteen swords saluted the triumph: eleven behind me and two to my right and left.[*1]

And while the swords received the blue rays that fell from the Cone, an extraordinary vision appeared to me: in front of me, behind the witnesses wrapped in black silk and above the pale glow of the candelabra, a silhouette formed, a black silhouette that had my shape and whose face resembled mine.

I looked at this phantom, asking myself if it was me, and I noticed that its torso suddenly grew exceedingly. It took the triangular form of our parade shields, but it was at least four times larger.

The arms of the phantom also became enormously extended,

---

[*]There are many things that can be said about this Second Degree initiation ritual. One of the most important is that when it was published (in late 1932), it had never actually taken place within the Confrérie de la Flèche d'Or. It is likely that it never took place in Naglowska's lifetime. Not only did she lack a place to do it, but she did not even have First Degree members (just two of them, "baptized" together) until February 5, 1935. If she envisaged a three-year period of "sweeping the Court," as indicated here, she would not have had time to raise anybody to the Second Degree, since she died in April 1936. Though this ritual, which is a variant of one called *l'équerre magique* (the magic square), may never have been performed, it is likely that other variants of the "magic square" were. The exact date of the First Degree "baptism," February 5, 1935, is given by Pierre Geyraud (anagrammatic pseudonym of Abbé Guyader, a Catholic priest with an interest in ancient and pagan religions) in Pierre Geyraud, *Les Petites Églises de Paris*.

powerful arms the hands of which were lost in infinity. They seemed, those arms, to be able to wrap themselves around the Universe!

I looked then at the head that resembled me, and I saw its green gaze, metallic, cold. It was not mine.

Above this gaze a large forehead rose. It was black, but it shone like gold. The Lunar Crescent crowned it with its two sharp points.

I would not know how to describe the strange light that surrounded this head with a resplendent aura. It contained the fire of all diamonds, but the folds of its vibrating waves were black.

It was the emanation of the Virile Force of the No.

I believed that Satan* said something to me, but there was nothing. The troubling silence of the Temple was interrupted by the ten calm voices of the witnesses who declared, "He has seen it."

Immediately, the Venerable Warriors and the Free Hunters lined up behind me in a semicircle answered, "May this triumph be propitious for him."

"May his Light be pure at the hour of the morn," said the Chief, and my old Guide, in front of him, added, "At the brief hour of the triumph of the No!"

"May the Star be ready at the exact minute!" shouted then the Guardian of the Temple, standing alone outside the triple circle formed around the round table.

"Present!" shouted the thirty-six Brothers, and I was one of their number.

---

*The embodiment of the Force of the No, above, which in its turn represents the discipline of control of sexual energy (in this case, "remaining dry to the end").

There was then a tremendous uproar in the vast arena, the provenance of which was not at all real. I heard the noise of chains falling on pavements, of floods overflowing riverbanks, of thunderbolts destroying walls, of houses crashing to the ground. Human voices let out atrocious cries, and animals seemed to flee a disaster.

I saw nothing, but I knew that all that was the Terrible Foreboding.

I had been well enough instructed to know the horrible struggle of the Yes and the No, the brief triumph of the latter, and the prolonged Victory of the affirmation of Life. For three years I had conscientiously belonged to the Court of the Knights of the Golden Arrow, where the members submitted themselves to the first discipline, of which the final goal was the Hanging, that is to say, the overturning of the Supreme Male Perfection,* attained at the cost of superhuman tests.

The vulgar man cannot understand these things, for the pivot of his life rests upon his personal interest, but the Free Hunters and, above all, the Venerable Warriors of our Confraternity know that to live for Satan† means to live for the Star . . . for the radiant Morning Star, who bends the human river back upon itself and obliges it to retake the Way of the Eternal Triangle,‡ in conformity to the Law. And when one knows what sacrifice is for, it becomes easy.

---

*Control of the sexual energy.

†The Force of the No, in this case representing control of sexual energy.

‡A point not to be missed in all this is that the Eternal Triangle, explained by Naglowska, is also emblematic of the pubic triangle, one of the most ancient symbols of the Feminine.

THE SACRED
SPECTACLE AND
THE WATER DANCE

The true testimony of the Free Hunter of the Court of Obedience of the Knights of the Golden Arrow continues thus:

When the phantom of Satan was absorbed by the intense blue rays of the Cone, the Brothers reestablished order in the vast arena of the Temple.

The incomparable Woman was again extended upon the three silk cushions, in the middle of the round table, and covered to the throat with a translucent silk of pure white.

The Guardian of the Temple extracted from the base of the double-walled screen the votive lamp that had been hidden there, which now burned with a Sacred Fire lit by the electrical emanation that had come from the blond head at the precise instant of the phallic operation described above. With a thousand precautions, he placed it on a gilded tripod at the bedside of the sleeper.

Invited by the formal gesture of the Guardian of the Temple, the Venerable Warriors and the Free Hunters climbed in single file up the narrow steps of the staircase that led to the galleries and installed themselves, each in his place, in two rows, one above the other: the Free Hunters lower, the Venerable Warriors above.

I occupied the place that was designated for me at the left entry of the first row. I had again put on my black Free Hunter costume, but I still didn't have my Bow and my Arrows, because my Dawn had not yet smiled.

Then, the sacred spectacle began.

Around the round table, where the splendid creature was sleeping, the circle formed by the candelabras had returned to the shadows because the Candles had burned down to the end and because there was no other light in the arena but the blue light of the Star of the Cone. The latter was also tinted with green and had noticeably dimmed.

An orchestra of harps, invisible as the orchestra of trumpets and hunting horns had been at the beginning of the session, played very sweet music that reminded one of the lapping of water on silent shores.

From time to time, the distant sound of a violin mixed in with repeating arpeggios of the harps, and it was then like waking up from a dream in the last hours of the night.

That lasted quite a while, not from the point of view of clock time, but as a sensation that prolonged the minutes.

The Water Dance

All of a sudden there was a soft sound to the right of the arena, also to the right of the sleeper, of whom we mainly saw the head graced with beautiful hair, and whose body covered in thin material followed the axis of the arena leading from the center of our two galleries to the entry door whose resistance I had broken when I entered the Sanctuary.

The sound continued, becoming confused with the undulating ripples of the harps, and thirty-five graceful dancers glided into the Temple through the small side door, so little elevated above the floor that a normal body would have to bend in two to clear it. Each dancer took two small steps before straightening up, and immediately resumed the bent-over pose a yard further on. When they straightened up, these women of graceful figure threw back their heads and their arms behind them, and when they bent themselves toward the ground, they touched the floor with the ends of their slender fingers.*[1]

This undulating march gave the effect of sea waves alternately swelling and subsiding to the rhythm of the languorous arpeggios.

This was the water dance, the art of which the women who are consecrated to the Temple of the Knights of the Golden Arrow learn as a religious duty.

The costume of these dancer-priestesses was composed of a thin dress of white silk, falling to the ankle, but slit up to the waist on each side.

---

*The first description of this dance was given by Naglowska in "Une Séance Magique," *La Flèche Organe d'Action Magique*. There she described it somewhat more acrobatically, with the women bending as far backward as they bent forward.

Thus the beautiful legs often appeared, in all their touching nudity.

The upper part of the body, from the waist to the shoulder, was hardly covered, and a wide green ribbon went twice around abdomen and buttocks, molding their forms. The ribbon was tied in a large butterfly knot on the left hip.

All our priestesses had very long hair, for they were chosen that way, and all were blondes, because the Morning Star cannot come from the mixed races, nor from the southern races. The Morning Star belongs to the arctic region of the north.*

Brown-haired and black-haired women should not be offended, for this is a Law, and human preferences will not change anything.

Nothing is due to human pleasure, and each race has its duty and its crowning.†

On the forehead of each of our dancers there shone a beautiful five-pointed star in diamonds. It was retained by a narrow golden ribbon, attached behind the nape of the neck over the falling flood of scattered hair. Under the pale, greenish glow of the Cone, its fires seemed silvered.

The undulating priestesses made a tour around the large arena.

---

*This sounds racist, but we have to bear in mind the time in which Naglowska lived. There has been a lot of Messianic mythology connected with "the north." Some of it probably comes from biblical passages such as Isaiah 41:25:

> I have raised up one from the north, and he is come: from the rising of the sun, and he shall call upon my name: and he shall come upon princes as upon mortar, and as the potter treads clay.

†Perhaps this statement goes some way toward compensating for the earlier one.

They approached the round table, forming a semicircle in front of our galleries.

Then the music became more penetrating, and the violin took the lead in playing a melody full of mystical dreams.

The priestesses held themselves straight now and advanced toward the table with an imperceptible step, extending their semicircle to form a perfect circle. They held their arms out in such a way that their fingers touched at the height of their shoulders.

They crossed the extinguished circle of candelabras, raising their knees to the waist, and stopped at the edge of the wood upon which my Lover reposed.

They then made some ritual gestures, wisely conforming to the rules of their intricate Art; and, guessing the propitious moment by the serious notes of the violin, they all turned at the same time, stooped down, and each grasped the needed candelabra.

Each priestess knew her candelabra, as she knew the Knight to whom it belonged by virtue of the holy and wholesome phallic operation by which she had been consecrated to the Satanic* Temple of the Order of the Golden Arrow, as I had just done for my Lover.[2]

The dancer-priestesses then proceeded to the collection of the sacred flame lit on this night.

From the large knot that decorated her left hip, each one took

---

*As a critic pointed out at the time, this "Satan" seems moral and almost virtuous. *"Le lecteur n'a rien à craindre . . . Satan y prend une forme morale—presque vertueuse."* "The reader has nothing to fear . . . there Satan takes a moral form—almost virtuous."

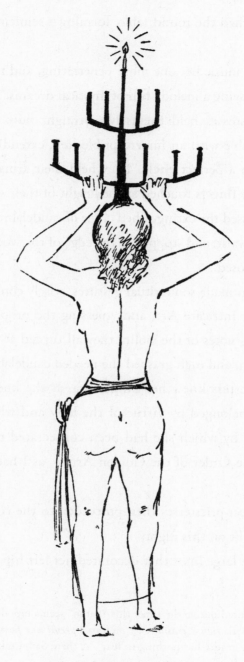

The Sacred Candlestick

the small lamp that was hidden there, and one after the other, approaching the burning lamp on the tripod, each lit her wick from it.

With a graceful and well-studied gesture, they fixed the lamps upon the candelabras, in the special place for the top Candle, and raising these sacred candlesticks above their heads, with their arms slightly bent, they left silently, to the slow rhythm of the music, in the direction of the side door located across from that by which they had entered.

This doorway was of normal size, and the two door panels were opened by the Guardian of the Temple, who had come down in time from his place in the second gallery for this passage of the Lovers into the chapel where no man ever went.

In this chapel, the priestesses of the Order of the Knights of the Golden Arrow maintained the Sacred Fire, renewed each time that a Sweeper was freed from obedience to the Court.

The Guardian of the Temple remained immobile, sword raised, while the thirty-five priestesses crossed, one by one, the threshold of the chapel, their gazes lowered as if they did not see him at all.

The door was not closed again after the procession, and I saw that the beautiful Lovers put their candelabras down in front of thirty-five oil paintings reproducing with a perfect likeness the features and silhouettes of my Brothers, the Free Hunters and the Venerable Warriors of the Order of the Golden Arrow, who were sitting with me in the two galleries.

I also saw that one portrait, mine, did not have its Holy Flame, certainly because my Lover was still asleep. Besides, my candelabra, of which the Candles were not lit during the banquet, still rested on the floor near the round table.

The dancer-priestesses knelt down, each one in front of the portrait of her Lover, Hunter or Warrior, and remained in deep meditation for several minutes.

The music then became very tender, and the violin sang religiously.

But suddenly there was a brusque change. The green light had mauve tints, the arpeggios of the harps became noisier, and the religious song of the violin, alone until then, supported now by the altos, passed through soft modulations to a dance tune, which soon had the rhythm of a waltz.

The thirty-five young women, light as gazelles, jumped to their small feet and ran, smiling and animated, into the grand hall of the Temple, whose arena they invaded with their mad rounds of two, three, and four, like a joyful spring whirlwind.

It stayed that way during a long quarter of an hour, and the light that illuminated the arena, falling from the height of the Cone, became more and more mauve, at times with violet stripes.

The green of the Night gave way, because the Dawn was near.

It smiled at last at my impatience!

The dancers noticed it before we did. They abruptly stopped their dance and hurried, like small radiant clouds, toward the round table where the symbolic Sun rose.

They helped the beautiful sleeper to sit up on her cushions. I did not see her pretty face, for she turned her back to us. I saw only her splendid hair with supple golden waves, which were caressed at this moment by the most ardent violet rays from the Star of the Cone.

Very quickly, the small hands of the thirty-five dancers went to work, and they dressed the Newly Born in the sacerdotal costume which I have described above.

To the sound of the harps and violins, my incomparable Lover appeared in all her beauty, led by her sisters before the judging stand of the thirty-six Knights of the Order of the Golden Arrow, and when she stopped at a distance of several steps in front of me, offering me her arms and her smile, I was on my feet with a bound.

I opened my jacket with a calculated movement, and bringing the two sides out to the beginning of the sleeves, I opposed to my seductive Woman my red-clad chest with the black motto: NO!

There was an instant of consternation in the music and in the group of thirty-six women, but quickly the Elder Sister, passing a bow and an arrow to the Younger, said to her:

"Shoot this arrow into his Heart."

"Yes, yes, shoot the arrow," cried the other sisters.

The Newly Born took the bow and the small golden arrow, aimed without trembling, and struck me full in the chest. But I held the arrow with my right hand, and it did me no harm.

I rebuttoned my jacket and stuck the arrow into my belt.

"There are more of them!" said the women, showing me the quiver.

My Lover held out her arm to seize the quiver, but the main entry door suddenly opened, and the grayness of the Morning overpowered in a second the mauve illusions of the Night.

A hunting horn gave the wakeup call, and the choir of trumpets answered it, dissipating the charm of the feminine magic.

The Guardian of the Temple seized a whip and cracked it three times.

The women let the bow and the quiver fall to the ground and hurried toward their chapel.

None of them returned, except the Newly Born, who caressed me yet with a long and resigned look. She then gathered up my candelabra, of which no Candle had yet burned, replaced the thirteenth Candle with the votive lamp placed on the tripod, and went, like the others, in the direction of the women's chapel. Like the others, she did not turn around.

I saw her cross the threshold of the Sanctuary of the Flame, holding over her head the fire that I had lit.

"May this separation be propitious for you!" my Brothers shouted. "And may the link established between her and you last eternally."

"So that his Work may triumph!" shouted the Guardian.

"So that we may accomplish our duty," answered the Chief.

"Present!" thundered the thirty-six male voices.

Then the Guardian of the Temple closed the door of the

The White Chargers

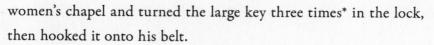

women's chapel and turned the large key three times* in the lock, then hooked it onto his belt.

He gathered up the bow, the arrows, and the quiver, which the priestesses had allowed to fall to the ground, and, presenting these symbols of the struggle† to me, he said to me:

"This will be your weapon, until the Final Victory."

"Until the Hanging," I answered.

"Until the Test of the Eagle," said the Freedmen.

"Until the Redirecting of the Human Tide onto the Great Way wished by Life," clarified the Warriors.

Then I descended into the gray arena, and the Guardian of the Temple fixed to my left shoulder the golden cord that keeps the quiver on the right hip, and the bow of the Free Hunters of obedience to the Court of the Knights of the Golden Arrow.

The hunting horns and the invisible trumpets saluted this event with a Warrior tune of full and vibrant sonority.

The Chief, followed by the procession of Venerable Warriors and Free Hunters, came down to where we were, and all the Brothers shook hands cordially.

I looked through the open door, and I saw in the courtyard thirteen White Chargers whose impatience was bridled by thirteen Sweepers.

---

*The key is always turned three times. This may be symbolic of the Sacred Triangle.
†The struggle between the Yes and the No.

He who shall have subdued the White
Charger, symbol of sex in its wild state,
that one shall be recognized as
Master in the kingdom of Life.

AUGUSTE APÔTRE*

---

*Again, in spite of the imaginary description in *La Flèche* 12, this is another of Naglowska's pseudonyms. The name apparently comes from *La Cinéide, ou la vache reconquise,* a national heroicomic epic poem from Belgium. The poem, written by Charles de Weyer de Streel in 1854, is about the famous thirteenth-century "War of the Cow." It is full of the false rhymes that Naglowska often used in her own poetry. It contains the following line in its twenty-third canto:

Ainsi, l'auguste apôtre allait de rangs en rangs
Elevant vers le ciel l'âme des combattants.

Appendix A

EYEWITNESS ACCOUNTS

"I HAVE ONLY ONE DREAM, YOU SEE, TO SAY THE GOLDEN MASS . . ."

Donald Traxler

Fortunately, we have some eyewitness accounts from people who attended Naglowska's sessions and conferences. Some of these were students of hers, others journalists or writers on esoteric and occult subjects. While each of the witnesses may be presumed to have had his own personal biases, taken together they give us a wonderful picture of Maria de Naglowska herself and the meetings and rituals at which she presided.

Chronologically, the earliest of these witnesses is René Thimmy (pseudonym of Maurice Magre, a French occultist), who sometimes worked as a journalist. His book, *La Magie à Paris,* was published in 1934.[1] He called Naglowska "Vera Petrouchka" and apparently interviewed her. He mentioned her smoking, as did others. She was petite, respectably dressed, with no trace of cosmetics on her face; he said you could pass her a hundred times without noticing her. He described her hair as ash blonde, cut short. Everything in her breathes propriety, he said. Just one characteristic detail in her physiognomy: her eyes. "It is difficult to forget them if they have come to rest on you once." He said that her eyes were blue, like glaciers or like the blades of daggers, lively and mobile, and illuminated by a fire coming from within. Among many other things, she told him that she needed a hall that was entirely her own, and he quoted her as saying, "I have only one dream, you see, to say the Golden Mass . . ."[2]

The next witness after Thimmy is "Pierre Geyraud," the anagrammatic pseudonym of l'Abbé Guyader, a Catholic priest. One would have expected him to be antagonistic, but actually he is rather evenhanded in his treatment of Naglowska. His book, *Les Petites Églises de Paris,* was published in 1937.[3] He interviewed her in her small hotel room, with her sitting on her bed. He described her as having an intelligent forehead under blonde hair, with eyes of a strange blue-green, singularly deep and lively. He said that an astonishing chastity radiated from her person (probably not what he expected, considering the rites that she was said to practice). Most importantly, though, Geyraud gives us a very detailed account of the First Degree initiation ritual of Claude d'Ygé and another of Naglowska's students (who later turned out to be Marc Pluquet). It is clear from the account that Geyraud already knew d'Ygé, a young poet and student, and he probably got some of the details of the "hymns" and the "baptism certificate" from him after the ceremony. In the 1970s the other inductee, Marc Pluquet, came

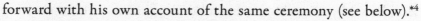

forward with his own account of the same ceremony (see below).*[4]

Another member of Naglowska's group, Henri Meslin, wrote a book under the name of B. Anel-Kham, which came out in 1938.[5] He tells us of a "splendid ceremony" during which two young women were consecrated as Priestesses of Love, with journalists present.[6] (We later learn, from Marc Pluquet, who at least one of the young women was.) Though Meslin must have been an eyewitness to many other things as well, most of his account is drawn from material published in *La Flèche*. He says, "As one can see, this curious doctrine regulates the intimate relations of the couple, spiritualizes love while keeping its sexual character, and to sum up, synthesizes the yonic and phallic cults in one."[7] "According to Maria de Naglowska, the gate of Heaven is opened by sacred coitus."[8]

A very important observer was Julius Evola, but he apparently didn't write about his involvement until about 1969, the year in which his book *Metafisica del sesso* was published. It was translated in the United States as *The Metaphysics of Sex* in 1983.[9] It is believed by many that Evola and Naglowska were lovers in the 1920s, when she was living in Rome, so he must have at least known a lot about her. What he wrote about her religious and magical practice in the early 1930s, though, seems to come from secondary sources. We

---

*In a way, one could say that there is a third version of this ceremony, because Gareth J. Medway, in his book *Lure of the Sinister: The Unnatural History of Satanism*, recently mistranslated Geyraud's account of it. Apparently he thought that *"se dresse devant l'assistance"* (stands up in front of the audience) meant "they assisted her to dress," thereby jumping to the conclusion that she had disrobed! This in turn led him to translate *"à reculons,"* which means "with backward steps," as "disrobing." But Naglowska was not nude in either of the historical accounts of this ritual, or indeed in any account we have of any other ritual.

do know that Naglowska translated a Dadaist poem by Evola into French in the 1920s, the only form in which it has survived. Evola also contributed an article to the first issue of Naglowska's little newspaper, *La Flèche*.[10] On the subject of Naglowska's teachings and her purported Satanism, Evola had this to say: "Even though it may not seem so, there is something more here than mere fantasy (quite apart from the inevitable 'Satanic,' which is absolutely out of place here)."[11]

The last of our witnesses, Marc Pluquet, is really the most important of all. In 1984 he wrote a biography of Maria de Naglowska, *La Sophiale*.[12] He was apparently her favorite student, and he in turn was very attached to her. He called her his spiritual mother. He tells who the other members of the group were (these included Jean Carteret, Camille Bryen, Henri Meslin, Claude d'Ygé, and others). I believe that "Marc Iver," whom Pluquet calls a friend of Naglowska,[13] was actually Marc Hiver, a Montparnasse art critic who was somewhat influential in the middle 1920s. By 1930 he had fallen out of fashion (due to his traditionalism), but he may have been the Maecenas who helped Maria start *La Flèche*. Pluquet tells us charmingly how Maria went every afternoon to the church of Notre-Dame des Champs for a period of reflection or meditation, and how he, Pluquet, always accompanied her, although sitting in the church bored him. He gives a good and detailed account of the ceremony at which he and Claude d'Ygé became Sweepers of the Court (Initiates of the First Degree). Pluquet also tells us about the ceremony where two young women (one of whom was Jane Pigkis, his wife) were ordained as postulants to be Priestesses of Love.[14] At the end of 1935 Naglowska told Pluquet that her mission was finished, and that she would soon be leaving. He was devastated (more so, he said, than he had been when his own mother had died). Maria also told him that nothing would be able to be done about spreading her teachings until two or three generations had passed.[15] If Naglowska's teachings did not completely disappear from the Earth, it is mostly thanks to her faithful student, Marc Pluquet.*

---

*I say this mainly because, as he tells us on page 17, he was instrumental in getting Naglowska's works republished during the 1970s. I have no information about these editions, but they must have been small ones, because the books are still very hard to find. He also tried, during and after the war, to get Naglowska's group started again. Due to the war and his own later financial reversals, these efforts did not come to anything.

Appendix B

"MASCULINE SATANISM, FEMININE SATANISM"

Translator's Note: In early 1933, perhaps stung by the criticism of a reviewer who had said that her Satan was "moral" and "almost virtuous,"[1] Naglowska wrote an article that went a long way toward explaining what she meant by "Satan" and "Satanism."[2] Because of its importance, I've included my translation of the complete article below.

People ask me if I present myself before the public as a disciple of P. B. Randolph, the celebrated American author of *Magia Sexualis*. Several serious occultists do. Here is my precise answer to this question: No, I am not a disciple of Randolph, for I am announcing a new religion in the world, whose revelation was given to me (not

by a human mouth, nor by books) at Rome, at the exact moment when the cardinals meeting at the Vatican received from the *Celestial Messenger* the inspiration for the election of the present Pope. I have already recounted that, in one of the numbers of the earlier series of *La Flèche*. This revelation, which I translated into human words in my recent volume *La Lumière du Sexe,* is not formally in contradiction with certain principles and procedures revealed in *Magia Sexualis,* but the Light by which I guide myself is not that by which Randolph guided himself. I ask my contradictors to please remember this point, because its importance is enormous. While Randolph, still bathing himself in Hindu idolatry, believes, as theosophists of all nuances do, in the independent and individual life and evolution of each soul particle—a concept that leads in the last analysis to dreadful reinforcement of the spiritual egotism of men and women—I rise up with all my energy, because such is the Divine Teaching that has been given to me, against this disastrous idea, erroneous and generator of all the evils of humankind. I say, and I ask that one take note, that nothing is personal or individual, *either on Earth, or in the Heavens, or in the waters under the Earth* (may those who have ears hear!). I say: nothing is opposite to me, and I am not opposite to anything, or anyone, and among you who read me, no one is opposite to anything, or to anybody separate from you, and no thing, no being, celestial or terrestrial, is opposite to you. We are not going toward Unity, we are Unity and have been since the beginning, which never happened. The idea of the separation of the self-styled particles of the Universe is an illusion of

Masculine Satanism,* and P. B. Randolph, just as all Theosophists, all Catholic theologians, all Jewish rabbis, and all educated people in general, supports, as is just, a kind of Masculine Satanism. The head of the male, Reason, belongs to Satan, as we have said. It is Masculine Satanism that pushes away direct Divine Revelation and passes through the sieve of negating examination of every Truth spontaneously shining forth from the life force. Masculine Satanism creates separation because it is separation, but its creation is fallacious. It is the No that opposes the Yes, and it dies without ceasing, for it is deprived of life. Meanwhile it is necessary, for it is the ferment that hosts life and without the struggle Life would not be. Since the beginning, which never was, the Elohim, the Yes and the No, have opposed Heaven to the Earth, confirming thus the principle of contrasts, which is the essential and profound basis of what is, of the Unique which is and which we are. Until the end, which will never come, the Elohim, the Yes and the No, will continue their great solitary combat, their universal combat, which is translated everywhere and which forms everything. Consequently, error will subsist, and illusion and Death will not cease. Masculine

---

*Naglowska seems here to be including in her definition of "Satanism" anything other than the nondualist position that she has just expressed. She seems to feel that the notion of "separation" is, in itself, Satanic. This is an extraordinary statement, and it clearly shows how wide the gulf is between Naglowska's definition of "Satanism" and ours. None of the people she mentions are worshippers of Satan, and neither is she. In fact, as a nondualist, she cannot even conceive of a Satan outside of the Self. If the examples Naglowska gives, Theosophists, Catholic theologians, Jewish rabbis, and educated people in general, represent "Satanism," then what does she mean by the term? It seems, on the face of it, as though the word *Satanism* could be replaced by *metaphysics, theology, religio-philosophical thinking,* or perhaps even *rational discourse.*

Satanism is immortal. It is immortal in the Heavens, it is immortal on Earth, it is immortal in the waters under the Earth. If the Death that it generates were to stop, Life would cease. Now Life cannot die. And because Life is, Death persists. Open your ears, serious and puffed-up-with-pride occultists, and try to understand this Truth . . .

But in Satan there is also the feminine side. This is quiet most of the time, because since the beginning words have been taken away from it. Sometimes God lets it speak, but only at the times when the suffering becomes too great, and then it is the song of the swan. A time finishes then, and another time begins, just because Feminine Satanism* has expressed itself. Feminine Satanism is the principle of the New Birth, and its cry of joy announces the new day. The Word is born then in the chaste womb of the Woman; it rises to her head and speaks through her mouth, determining the beginning of a New Era. Feminine Satanism generally keeps quiet, because it is the Guardian of the Threshold, the silent Guardian that opposes the solar phallus to prevent fecundation. It is its assignment to oppose fertilization, the joy of the Sun, because without this opposition, Life would not be. But when the suffering becomes too great and the trials are too widespread, bending bodies that are too weak, the Guardian of the Threshold, Woman-Satan, Divine-Mother-Satan,[†] pronounces her Word. Then everything changes in the Heavens

---

*Maria's thought here may be made more accessible by replacing the word *Satanism* with the word *theology* or the word *philosophy*.

[†]In line with the foregoing, the word *Satan* in these compounds could probably be replaced by *theologian* or *philosopher*.

and on the Earth and in the waters under the Earth, and during a sublime instant, the separation no longer exists; the Man and the Woman are not more than a single thing, the two contraries are dissolved into a single One, the cry of joy resounds, salvation arrives, and Life triumphs.

We know that the following promise has been given to the Just: *the Woman will crush the head of the malefic Serpent at the appointed hour.* Now, this is what I do. I crush the head of the Serpent, Masculine Satanism, and I proclaim the triumph of the Solar Shaft* in the mouth of Feminine Satanism.† There you have the difference between my teaching and that of Randolph, all the theosophists, all the theologians, and all the rabbis. I proclaim the triumph of Life,‡ because of the joy of the Guardian of the Threshold. This joy is spiritual, for it comes from the transformation of the waters of Hell into the streams of Heaven.

And now, may the learned director of *L'Astrosophie* of Carthage reread me. May the venerable bishop of the Gnostic Church at Lyon, who asks if my teaching is traditional, reread me. May the occultist booksellers, who refuse my book in their shops, reread me. May the shameless sexologists, who preach the dissoluteness of women, repent. May the doctors who understand nothing about it, but who engage in sexual philosophy just the same, blush in shame, for they

---

*The phallus.
†The terms Masculine Satanism and Feminine Satanism evidently include metaphysics, religion, philosophy, and perhaps all rational processes.
‡ = God.

are committing the sin against the Spirit, the only one that will not be pardoned, for they prevent all understanding of Truth and cast humankind into mortal debauchery. They would do well to be silent, for Truth shines forth and will confound them soon . . .

Today is the brief instant of the triumph of Truth. Hasten if you wish to enjoy it. When the instant has passed, the Lie will return, the Lie of the comments.* Then it will be too late. The elect, those who shall have merited it, will enter into the new Temple, and the others will be crushed under the ruins of collapsed houses.†

---

*The French word used, *commentaire,* can also mean "criticism," and that is probably how it should be understood here.
†Naglowska may here be referring to the catastrophe of the Second World War, which she foresaw and publicly predicted in 1935,[3] or else to a disaster not yet come.

Appendix c

A PREVIEW OF *THE HANGING MYSTERY*

Translator's Note: The Hanging Mystery *was published in French in 1934 under the title* Le Mystère de la Pendaison. *Below is a preview of that work, written by Maria de Naglowska.*

If you have read with attention, O fervent and restless disciple, the remarkable testimony of the Free Hunter of the Court of the Knights of the Golden Arrow, you must have understood many things.

If such is not the case, you are to blame, for whoever cannot understand the clear language of symbols* would not understand

---

*As mentioned in the translator's note at the beginning of this book, Naglowska herself recognized, a few months before she died, that her symbolism needed clarifying in accessible language "for awakened women and men who will not necessarily be symbolists."

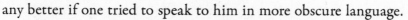

any better if one tried to speak to him in more obscure language.

The second Great Test, that which the Free Hunters undergo for purposes of their admission to the Corps of the Venerable Warriors, is as latent in the first as the seed of the rose in the newly formed bud.

It is still more impressive, and it demands an unprecedented courage on the part of the Man tested, unimaginable for the profane.

For, when the Free Hunter returns to the Temple, after the long Lion Hunt, which consists of mixing in with the tribulations of vulgar life without becoming stained, without compromising with the crowds, without falling into their snares, and without ever profiting personally from the enormous occult force* acquired at the Test of the Charger—he has decided to offer himself in sacrifice for the triumph of Life (= God), the Path of which he has made straight by his Negations.

At the moment of the terrible ceremony, the description of which we will give in this volume, he no longer sees Satan before him and separated from him by the protective circle of the witnesses, but he is himself Satan, himself the unlimited Force of Negation.

And he immolates himself, he accepts in his whole being, top to

---

*This "enormous occult force" is acquired through disciplined control of the sexual energy (represented by the White Charger). The control and utilization of sexual energy to achieve Illumination is really what Maria de Naglowska is about. Anyone who tries to ignore and pass over this part is simply missing her message. "In effect, the second initiation into the hermetic mysteries teaches us the Way to make use of the impetuous Charger, which is only a means of starting out on the Great Road."[1] "For the Charger must take us across the waters of the river of separation to the second life."[2] The Illumination at the end of that Great Road is the true Light of Sex.

bottom, the electrifying penetration of the luminous Feminine (religiously purified) at the sublime moment of sacred coitus, for which his Lover is awake.*

The Man comes away from this test shaken in his Reason, and he is then the Sublime Madman of which the secret scriptures speak.

For during this operation of high golden[†] magic, Satan (= Cosmic Reason that denies and doubts) is sent to Hell, that is to say into the sexual organ of the Man, and it is easy to believe the overwhelming effect that results.

When, after a period more or less prolonged, the one tested becomes calm and regains his equilibrium, he is really a new Man, and it is then that one invests him with the dignity of Venerable Warrior of the Golden Arrow.

The gifts and capacities that he possesses then are of such a nature that a profane person is frightened of them or does not believe in them, finding the thing superhuman; for every vulgar man is persuaded of his own perfection and takes offense if another surpasses him. It is because of this that the men and women of the crowd are condemned to mediocrity.

The ritual and the doctrine of the Knights of the Golden Arrow include all the pure pearls that one recovers in the great religions and in all the true secret traditions, for the Truth is One and every free person always sees the same Light.

---

*As opposed to asleep during the Second Degree initiation.

†This is a reference to Naglowska's planned Golden Mass, the celebration of which was to include ritual sexual intercourse.

But in our time, the Word that we pronounce is new, because outside of the true text published in this book everything is just commentary, and often false commentary. To avoid all troublesome misunderstandings, we cast our silence upon all the occultist literature written in these last years of the Dark Era that we are passing through and which will end soon, and we proclaim that there is not, and there will not be, any pact between us and the others. *New wine must be poured into new glasses.*

There is, besides that, a historical reason, and to explain we take up again the image of the human train that we gave in the first part of this volume.

In effect, the eternal course of humanity around the Divine Eye (p. 23) follows the triangular Way that composes itself and will always recompose itself in this same order: first the line of the Fall from the Summit to the Base, next the line of the Base, then that of the Ascension from the Base toward the Summit.

Accordingly as the human train is on one or another of these three lines, the revelation that is made in the spirit of those *freed from the misery of the crowds* is different, and the gifts acquired by those who pass the Great Tests at the moment of the Triumph of the Eagle, or the Vision of the Pure Sun, are others, because at each Angular Passage of the Triangle (the Cosmic Minutes!) another Hypostasis is projected upon the Earth.

At the Summit, it is the Vision of the Father. At the first Angle of the Base it is the Vision of the Son. At the second Angle of the Base it is the Vision of the Mother. But these Three are only One in Truth, and there is no truth in idolatrous conceptions. We have already said it.

In conformity to this immutable Law, the Man who is reborn in the Satanic* Temple at Midnight of the First Era proclaims the Truth of the Father. He rejects the Mother and her Sublime Childbirth, and imposes on humans a religion that is essentially reasonable, that is to say having Reason and, consequently, having Satan.[†]

The rule of such a religion reunites the faithful in the courtyard, only admits the intellectual elite into the arena of the Temple, and encloses in the Holy of Holies, visited once a year by the Supreme Chief of the priests, the Miraculous Rod reposing in the Symbolic Ship,[‡] which represents at the same time a distant Memory and an incomprehensible Hope.

The ethic of a religion of this type, which repeats each time that humanity is on the line of the Fall, rests on the principles of Justice and Balance. Women do not belong to the community except insofar as they procreate the species. The childless woman is damned.

When the First Day, to so characterize it, approaches its Noon, the fruit is mature and begins to rot. The spirit is extinguished and the commentary begins. It continues so, going from bad to worse, until Midnight.

Then the Man is reborn who sees the Son. He separates the Woman from the Man, for he wishes that all should be free. The faithful gather in the great arena, the courtyard no longer exists, and

---

*See appendix B.
†Who has been defined as Cosmic Reason.
‡The Rod and the Ship are also symbols of the sex organs.

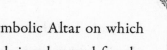

the Holy of Holies is transformed into a symbolic Altar on which a Mystery is accomplished, the goal of which is ephemeral for the Earth.

A new ethic is proclaimed: the ethic of brotherly charity, done with meekness and humility. It is no longer Reason that triumphs, but the Heart, whose reasons are subtle and contradictory. Women, in this day, must remain virgin to deserve Heaven, but there are some who give birth and those are *pardoned*!

Until Noon, until the new Midnight, this day blossoms, then it dies away. A new Dark Era intervenes and another Man is born at Midnight.

That one is reborn of the Woman duly purified in the Satanic* Temple. He is reborn from his triumphant Lover, after the Hanging.

He proclaims the Religion of the Third Term of the Trinity, and its Reign lasts as long as it must: from Midnight to the new Midnight.

And so it is eternally.

---

*See appendix B.

NOTES

FOREWORD.
MARIA DE NAGLOWSKA,
A PROTAGONIST OF SEXUAL MAGIC IN
THE EARLY TWENTIETH CENTURY

1. Wouter J. Hanegraaff and Jeffrey J. Kripal, eds., *Hidden Intercourse: Eros and Sexuality in the History of Western Esotericism* (Boston: Brill, 2008).

2. See www.esswe.org and www.aseweb.org.

3. Marc Pluquet, *La Sophiale: Maria de Naglowska: sa vie, son oeuvre* (Paris: OTO, 1993).

4. René Thimmy, *La Magie à Paris* (Paris: Les Éditions de France, 1934), 79.

5. Sarane Alexandrian, "Maria de Naglowska. Prophétesse de la Religion du Troisième Millénaire," *Supérieur Inconnu* no. 8, (October–November 1997): 11.

6. Gisèle Laurent, *Les sociétés secrètes érotiques* (Alger: Société de Publications et d'Éditions, 1961).

A NOTE ON THE TRANSLATION

1. Marc Pluquet, *La Sophiale* (Montpeyroux, France: Éditions Gouttelettes de Rosée, n. d.), 14.

INTRODUCTION

1. We know about Bryen from Pluquet, *La Sophiale,* 7; also cited in John Patrick Deveney and Franklin Rosemont, *Paschal Beverly Randolph: A Nineteenth-Century Black American Spiritualist* (Albany: SUNY Press, 1996), XVIII. In the foreword to the Deveney book, Rosemont also mentions Gengenbach's connection with Naglowska. Alexandrian's study of Naglowska is in Alexandrian, *Les libérateurs de l'amour* (Paris: Éditions du Seuil, 1977), 185–206. As an example of the difficulty of verifying the other names, the claim is made for both Bataille and Paulhan in Nikolas Schreck and Zeena Schreck, *Demons of the Flesh* (Clerkenwell, London: Creation Books, 2002), 278. Unfortunately the only supporting reference the Schrecks give for Naglowska is to an earlier article by Nikolas Schreck. Their bibliography does not include anything by Bataille, Paulhan, or Naglowska (although they mentioned Naglowska seventy-four times in their book), and the claim is not supported in any footnote or endnote. It must, therefore, be considered hearsay, at least for now. In the case of William Seabrook, his connections with Man Ray and Michel Leiris are well known and documented by both their and his own writings. Whether Seabrook did indeed attend these sessions is not proven as far as I am concerned. I have read his autobiography and the biography written by his second wife, Marjorie Worthington, and found nothing. The only indication that Seabrook was aware of Naglowska, other than his association with Man Ray and other surrealists, is in the Wambly Bald *Tribune* article cited here.

2. Pluquet, *La Sophiale,* 3–6.

3. Maria de Naglowska, "Mon chef spirituel," *La Flèche, Organe d'Action Magique* 10 (February 15, 1932): 2, 3.

4. Julius Evola, *The Metaphysics of Sex* (New York: Inner Traditions International, 1983), 261.

5. P. B. Randolph, *Magia Sexualis*, French translation by Maria de Naglowska (Paris: Robert Télin, 1931).

6. Pluquet, *La Sophiale,* 8, 14.

7. Maria de Naglowska, *Le Rite sacré de l'amour magique* (Paris: *Supplément de La Flèche Organe d'Action Magique,* 1932).

8. Maria de Naglowska, *La Lumière du sexe* (Paris: Éditions de la Flèche, 1932).

9. Maria de Naglowska, *Le Mystère de la pendaison* (Paris: Éditions de la Flèche, 1934).

10. Pluquet, *La Sophiale,* 12.

11. Maria de Naglowska, "Avant la Guerre de 1936," *La Flèche Organe d'Action Magique* 20 (January 15, 1935): 3.

12. Pluquet, *La Sophiale,* 14.

13. Ibid., 13.

CHAPTER 4. REASON

1. MacDonald and Margolese in *Fertility and Sterility* 1:26 (1950).

2. Maria de Naglowska, *La Flèche* 16 (March 15, 1933): 19.

CHAPTER 6. SEX

1. See Epiphanius, *Panarion,* Book 27; "La Flèche" (a pseudonym of Maria de Naglowska), "Le Livre de la Vie," *La Flèche, Organe d'Action Magique* 6 (March 15, 1931): 1.

2. Genesis 3:15 per Vulgate: *Inimicitias ponam inter te et mulierem et semen tuum et semen illius ipsa conteret caput tuum et tu insidiaberis calcaneo eius.*

CHAPTER 7. THE CALVARY OF REASON

1. Maria de Naglowska, "Une Séance Magique," *La Flèche* 12 (May 15, 1932): 2–3.

CHAPTER 8. THE WHITE CHARGER

1. Naglowska, "Une Séance Magique," *La Flèche* 12.

CHAPTER 10.
THE INITIATIC BANQUET
AND THE VIRILE TAPER

1. See René Thimmy, *La Magie à Paris,* 74–78; "Hanoum," "L'Équerre Magique (Nouvelle)," *La Flèche Organe d'Action Magique* 11 (March 15, 1932): 4–6; Pierre Geyraud, *Les Petites Églises de Paris* (Paris: Éditions Émile-Paul Frères, 1937), 153.

CHAPTER 11.
THE SACRED SPECTACLE
AND THE WATER DANCE

1. Naglowska, "Une Séance Magique," 3.
2. *L'Astrosophie* 8, no. 5 (January 21, 1933): 176.

APPENDIX A.
EYEWITNESS ACCOUNTS

1. René Thimmy, *La Magie à Paris* (Paris: Les Éditions de France, 1934), 63–81.
2. Ibid., 72.
3. Pierre Geyraud, *Les Petites Églises de Paris* (Paris: Éditions Émile-Paul Frères, 1937), 144–53.
4. Gareth J. Medway, *Lure of the Sinister: The Unnatural History of Satanism* (New York: New York University Press, 2001), 19.
5. B. Anel-Kham, *Théorie et pratique de la magie sexuelle* (Paris: Librairie Astra, 1938), 40–44.
6. Ibid., 40.
7. Ibid., 44.
8. Ibid., 40.
9. Julius Evola, *The Metaphysics of Sex* (New York: Inner Traditions International, 1983), 261–63.

10. J. Evola, "Occidentalisme," *La Flèche Organe d'Action Magique* 1 (October 15, 1930): 3–4.

11. Evola, *Metaphysics of Sex,* 263.

12. Pluquet, *La Sophiale.*

13. Ibid., 11.

14. Ibid., 13.

15. Ibid., 13.

APPENDIX B.
"MASCULINE SATANISM,
FEMININE SATANISM"

1. Unsigned review, "La Lumière du Sexe," *L'Astrosophie* 8, no. 5 (January 21, 1933): 176.

2. Maria de Naglowska, "Satanisme Masculin, Satanisme Féminin," *La Flèche Organe d'Action Magique* 16 (March 15, 1933): 20–24.

3. La Redaction, "Avant la Guerre de 1936," *La Flèche Organe d'Action Magique* 20 (January 15, 1935): 3.

APPENDIX C.
A PREVIEW OF
THE HANGING MYSTERY

1. La Flèche, "Le Coursier initiatique et le Cavalier sans peur" (The Initiatic Charger and the Fearless Rider), *La Flèche Organe d'Action Magique* 9 (January 15, 1932): 1–2.

2. Ibid.

BIBLIOGRAPHY

Alexandrian, Sarane. *Les libérateurs de l'amour.* Paris: Éditions du Seuil, 1977.

Anel-Kham, B. (pseudonym of Henri Meslin). *Théorie et pratique de la magie sexuelle.* Paris: Librairie Astra, 1938.

Deveney, John Patrick, and Franklin Rosemont. *Paschal Beverly Randolph: A Nineteenth-Century Black American Spiritualist.* Albany: SUNY Press, 1996.

Evola, Julius. *The Metaphysics of Sex.* New York: Inner Traditions International, 1983.

Geyraud, Pierre (pseudonym of l'Abbé Pierre Guyader). *Paris et lle de France histoire et régionale.* Paris: Éditions Émile-Paul Frères, 1937.

Hakl, Hans Thomas. "Maria de Naglowska and the Confrérie de la Flèche d'Or." *Politica Hermetica* 20 (2006): 113–23.

Naglowska, Maria de. *La Lumière du sexe.* Paris: Éditions de la Flèche, 1932.

———. *Le Mystère de la pendaison.* Paris: Éditions de la Flèche, 1934.

———. *Le Rite sacré de l'amour magique: Aveu 26.1.* Paris: *Supplément de La Flèche Organe d'Action Magique,* 1932.

———. Writings in *La Flèche Organe d'Action Magique* 1–20 (October 15, 1930–January 15, 1935).

Pluquet, Marc. *La Sophiale: Maria de Naglowska, sa vie—son oeuvre.* Montpeyroux, France: Éditions Gouttelettes de Rosée, n.d.

Randolph, Paschal Beverly (compiled and translated by Maria de Naglowska). *Magia Sexualis.* Paris: Robert Télin, 1931.

Schreck, Nikolas, and Zeena Schreck. *Demons of the Flesh.* Clerkenwell, London: Creation Books, 2002.

Thimmy, René. *La Magie à Paris.* Paris: Les Éditions de France, 1934.

INDEX

Page numbers in *italics* refer to illustrations.

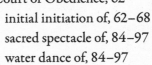

BOOKS OF RELATED INTEREST

The Complete Illustrated Kama Sutra
Edited by Lance Dane

Tantric Sex for Men
Making Love a Meditation
by Diana Richardson and Michael Richardson

Tantric Orgasm for Women
by Diana Richardson

Sexual Reflexology
Activating the Taoist Points of Love
by Mantak Chia and William U. Wei

Healing Love through the Tao
Cultivating Female Sexual Energy
by Mantak Chia

Taoist Foreplay
Love Meridians and Pressure Points
by Mantak Chia and Kris Deva North

The Complete Kama Sutra
The First Unabridged Modern Translation
of the Classic Indian Text
Translated by Alain Daniélou

Tantric Secrets for Men
What Every Woman Will Want Her Man to Know
about Enhancing Sexual Ecstasy
by Kerry Riley with Diane Riley

INNER TRADITIONS • BEAR & COMPANY
P.O. Box 388
Rochester, VT 05767
1-800-246-8648
www.InnerTraditions.com

Or contact your local bookseller